M&A Activity, Divestitures and Initial Public Offerings in the Fashion Industry

Corporate Finance and Governance

Herausgegeben von Dirk Schiereck

Band 8

PETER LANG
Frankfurt am Main · Berlin · Bern · Bruxelles · New York · Oxford · Wien

Steffen Meinshausen

M&A Activity, Divestitures and Initial Public Offerings in the Fashion Industry

PETER LANG
Internationaler Verlag der Wissenschaften

Bibliografische Information der Deutschen Nationalbibliothek
Die Deutsche Nationalbibliothek verzeichnet diese Publikation in der Deutschen Nationalbibliografie; detaillierte bibliografische Daten sind im Internet über http://dnb.d-nb.de abrufbar.

Zugl.: Darmstadt, Univ., Diss., 2012

Gedruckt auf alterungsbeständigem, säurefreiem Papier.

D 17
ISSN 1869-537X
ISBN 978-3-631-62110-3

www.peterlang.de

“I have heard with admiring submission the experience of the lady who declared that the sense of being perfectly well-dressed gives a feeling of inward tranquility which religion is powerless to bestow.“

(Ralph Waldo Emerson, *Letters and Social Aims*)

“One should either be a work of art, or wear a work of art.”

(Oscar Wilde, *Phrases and Philosophies for the Use of the Young*)

ACKNOWLEDGEMENTS

In achieving this academic endeavor, I would like to take the time to say thanks to a variety of people that have guided me throughout the process of writing my dissertation by giving me valuable feedback and helping me to shape my ideas in a constructive way. I really enjoyed my time as a PhD student and research assistant and would also like to thank many individuals that I met on various occasions during this particular period in time.

First, I would like to thank Prof. Dr. Dirk Schiereck for his great support and kind personality that have encouraged me to broaden my theoretical knowledge in the fields of corporate finance and behavioral economics. Over the last two and a half years, I have gained tremendous insights into empirical corporate finance research due to his professional mentoring and constructive feedback. I would also like to take the opportunity to thank him as well as my fellow PhD students Anit, Christian B., Christian T., Christoph, Daniel, Julian, Malte, Mehtap, Robert as well as Mrs. Felicitas Eichler for the great atmosphere during my time as a research assistant at the chair of corporate finance in Darmstadt.

There are many others who have contributed to this dissertation and my research papers, such as Prof. Dr. Joachim Ahrens for his support during my studies of business administration in Göttingen and Dr. Mark Mietzner at Darmstadt University of Technology. In addition, I thank various editors and reviewers at international journals that have commented on my papers and have always shown room for further improvement of my analyses.

I am also very grateful for being given the opportunity to present my research papers to international audiences of PhD students, professors and faculty members. First, I would like to thank Luis Rodríguez-Domínguez who reviewed my paper on accounting performance changes following fashion mergers for his constructive feedback at the 4th International Accounting & Finance Doctoral Symposium in Salamanca (Spain) in July 2011.

I also thank the audience at the 2011 Academy of Behavioral Finance and Economics in Los Angeles (USA) where I presented my paper on the causes of insolvency of German fashion manufacturer ESCADA AG and behavioral finance in September 2011. Finally, I also very much enjoyed the great time at the Academy of Economics and Finance in Charleston (USA) where I was given the opportunity to present my working paper on IPO performance in the fashion and leather accessories industry in early February 2012.

I also thank many great people at the investment banking division of Morgan Stanley in Frankfurt am Main for the very exciting and ultimately rewarding time during my internship in the fall of 2011. Special acknowledgements go to Daniel, Gloria, Raphael, Roman and Tjark for many late-night conversations, working sessions, dinners and nights out on the town.

Apart from all the great academic support these people have given me over the course of the last two and a half years, I will also not forget to say thanks to many great friends who have made life enjoyable at all times. There are too many people to mention, but special acknowledgements go to Benedikt Lohaus, Gero Schomann, Markus Ahlborn, Moritz Bergmann and Tommy Quansah for the great times I spent with them in Amsterdam, Berlin, Frankfurt, Göttingen, London, Munich and Münster.

Some people I met during my first year as an external PhD student in Berlin deserve further credit, such as my great colleagues at direktzu GmbH where I worked as a management assistant. I would also like to thank Ramona Brösamle for showing me many of Berlin's culinary highlights and Jan-Michael Granowski for the countless good times at Soho House Berlin.

Last, but not least, my deepest gratitude goes to my loving parents, Petra and Jürgen, and my grandmother Lydia for their lifelong support and encouragement. I highly value your incomparable commitment during every period of my life. I am very proud to dedicate this dissertation to you!

PREFACE

In vielen Industrien mit hoher Fusionsdynamik sind die Treiber der Konsolidierung recht klar zu erkennen. In einer derart heterogenen Industrie wie der Modewirtschaft mit großen Produzenten, reinen Einzelhändlern und selbst produzierenden Handelsketten fällt eine entsprechende Identifikation dagegen schwer. Die Industrie wird von weltweit bekannten großen Konglomeraten und Handelsketten dominiert, aber auch viele kleinere Unternehmen sind wohl bekannt und mehr noch die Marken, unter denen ihre Produkte vertrieben werden. Weniger bekannt sind dagegen die Eigentümerstrukturen von den Unternehmen, deren Marken allgegenwärtig erscheinen, und die Konsequenzen, die mit Veränderungen in der Eigentümerstruktur einhergehen.

Für die Unternehmen der Modeindustrie stellt sich unmittelbar eine ganze Reihe von fundamentalen Fragen. So fällt es schwer, die immanente, Wert schaffende Logik dieser konsolidierenden Industrie zu begreifen. Die Sicht von Produzenten und die gleichgerichtete Wahrnehmung durch die Kunden schließen bspw. wegen der selbst definierten Exklusivität von Luxusmodegütern Skaleneffekte in Produktion und Distribution vielfach aus, andere offensichtliche Fusionsvorteile drängen sich nicht auf. Andererseits fehlen aber gern zitierte Megafehlschläge von Fusionen, wie sie aus anderen Branchen wie der Automobilindustrie oder dem Bankensektor bekannt sind.

Auch hier setzt die Arbeit von Herrn Meinshausen an. Im Gegensatz zur Wertschätzung, die die Modeindustrie in vielen anderen Wissenschaftszweigen erfährt, stellt der Akademiker nämlich fest, dass die kapitalmarktorientierte finanzwirtschaftliche Forschung diesem Segment bislang recht wenig Beachtung geschenkt hat. Die Dissertationsschrift von Herrn Meinshausen betritt somit (erstaunlicherweise) wissenschaftliches Neuland. In mehreren empirischen Auswertungen und einer Fallstudie werden verschiedene Facetten der Modeindustrie zwischen Corporate Finance und Corporate Governance mit ihren Werttreibern und Risikoprofilen dokumentiert. Damit wird ein objektiver Kenntnisstand aufgebaut, auf dessen Basis sich fundierte Handlungsempfehlungen für die Gestaltung von Übernahmen und Börsengängen in der Modeindustrie ableiten lassen.

Herr Meinshausen kann die selbst gesetzten Ziele in seiner Dissertationsschrift bestens erfüllen. Die Arbeit enthält zahlreiche spannende Resultate und ist so geschrieben, dass es den Lesern Freude macht, sie bis zum Ende intensiv zu studieren. Ich wünsche der Arbeit eine ihr gebührende weite Verbreitung.

Professor Dr. Dirk Schiereck

CONTENTS

LIST OF FIGURES

LIST OF TABLES

LIST OF ABBREVIATIONS

Adj.	Adjusted
AOP	Abnormal operating performance
BHAR	Buy-and-hold abnormal returns
BHR	Buy-and-hold returns
BV	Book value
CAAR	Cumulative average abnormal returns
CAGR	Compound annual growth rate
Capex	Capital expenditure
CAR	Cumulative abnormal returns
CDAX	Composite DAX (see below: DAX)
CEO	Chief Executive Officer
CFO	Chief Financial Officer
DAX	Deutscher Aktienindex
DCF	Discounted cash flow
EBIT	Earnings before interest and taxes
EBITDA	Earnings before interest, taxes, depreciation and amortization
EV	Enterprise value
Exp.	Expense
FY	Fiscal year
IPO	Initial public offering
LVMH	LVMH Moët Hennessy – Louis Vuitton SA
M&A	Mergers and acquisitions
MV	Market value
No.	Number

Nobs	Number of observations
OCF	Operating cash flow
OLS	Ordinary least squares
P/E	Price/earnings
PDA	Personal digital assistant
PE	Private equity
Perf-matched	Performance-matched
PPR	Pinault-Printemps-Redoute SA
SEO	Seasoned equity offering
SIC	Standard Industrial Classification
VC	Venture capital
WTA	Willingness to accept
WTO	World Trade Organization
WTP	Willingness to pay

LIST OF SYMBOLS

α_j	Alpha of company *j* (OLS regression parameter α)
Adj. R^2	Adjusted R-squared (OLS coefficient of determination)
AR_{jt}	Abnormal return of company *j* on day *t*
β_j	Beta of company *j* (OLS regression parameter β)
$BHAR_{jm}$	Buy-and-hold abnormal return for company *j* in month *m*
BHR_{bm}	Buy-and-hold return of benchmark index *b* in month *m*
BHR_{jm}	Buy-and-hold return for company *j* in month *m*
CAR_j	Cumulative abnormal return of company *j*
Σ	Summation operator
€bn(m)	Billions (millions) of euros
ε_{jt}	Residual disturbance term
$E(R_{jt})$	Expected return of company *j* on day *t*
N	Sample size
Π	Product operator
R_{bm}	Return of benchmark index *b* in month *m*
R_{bt}	Return of benchmark index *b* on day *t*
R_{jm}	Return of company *j* in month *m*
R_{jt}	Return of company *j* on day *t*
$Ratio^{ind\text{-}adj}_{post,\,j}$	Industry-adjusted post-merger financial ratio of company *j*
$Ratio^{ind\text{-}adj}_{pre,j}$	Industry-adjusted pre-merger financial ratio of company *j*
$bn(m)	Billions (millions) of US dollars
$[t_1; t_2]$	Event window ranging from days t_1 to t_2
x	Multiplier (e.g. for EV/EBIT multiple, market-to-book ratio)

1 INTRODUCTION

This dissertation analyzes the implications of mergers and acquisitions, divestiture activities and initial public offerings in the fashion and leather accessories industry. It contains four independent empirical studies and covers a large fraction of corporate finance-related activity in a business segment that has been widely disregarded in previous research. The purpose of this introduction is to give a short overview on macroeconomic trends and industry-specific characteristics of the apparel industry. We will also briefly introduce our four research objectives and some of the key findings of our following studies.

Generally, the apparel business segment has seen extensive shifts in industry dynamics over the course of the previous decades. High labor costs in established Western countries and decreasing costs of global logistics have triggered a wide-spread outsourcing of manufacturing activities into low-cost developing countries. This has rendered a great deal of workers in developed countries unemployed. The subsequent reductions in manufacturing costs and mass production have also given way to the strong proliferation of clothes in the low-price segment (Abernathy et al. (1995)). Still, European and North American apparel companies play leading roles in the up-scale and luxury fashion sector where the main emphasis is rather put on product quality, individual features and exclusivity than price competition (Glasmeier et al. (1993)).

Aggregate demand has further shifted from traditional developed to emerging markets such as China, India, the countries of the Middle East and Russia where increases in economic wealth and personal prosperity in particular fuel the aspiration for clothing and related products. An empirical study by KPMG (2009) has shown that individuals in these countries are especially prone to the consumption of luxury goods and upscale fashion, resulting in strong growth rates and steadily increasing market shares of these business segments.

In addition, distribution characteristics have changed on a large scale due to the fashion industry's strong affiliation to product sales via the internet and web-based applications. Gertner and Stillman (2001) have shown empirically that apparel products are among the best-selling items for online distribution in the United States. The acquisition of internet retailer Net-A-Porter.com by Swiss luxury conglomerate Richemont in 2010 has further underlined the importance online distribution nowadays carries for fashion and accessories companies.

The fashion industry is now both a multi-billion dollar business sector as well as a fast-growing market segment. According to recent international trade statistics of the World Trade Organization, the apparel and textiles industry has accounted for $527bn or 4.3% of the world's trade volume in 2009 while growing at an impressive CAGR of 5.0% over the course of the years 2000 to 2009 (WTO (2010)). Given the fact that even more upcoming economies are gaining access to fashion and luxury products, it is reasonable to believe that the apparel industry is facing many years of sustainable growth in the near future.

Besides these favorable macroeconomic developments, the industry itself has changed due to consolidation and alternating customer demands. Many companies that headed the fashion "zeitgeist" of a certain era have become irrelevant and have been replaced by fashion houses and designers that were able to better understand current lifestyles. The fast-paced rhythm of the two collections-driven business model is a distinctive characteristic that differentiates the fashion segment from other industries with more long-term oriented product life cycles. Fashion businesses are therefore forced to implement permanent innovation and adaptation to their ever-changing industry dynamics.

Like many other industries, the fashion segment has seen a tremendous amount of M&A activity in previous decades. The luxury goods sector which also includes many luxury fashion brands has become especially concentrated with the four European conglomerates LVMH, PPR, Compagnie Financière Richemont and Swatch Group now being the predominant worldwide players. In the leather accessories segment, Mariella Burani Fashion Group has acquired a large portfolio of handbag and similar leather product manufacturers. On a remarkable note, all of these companies are located in Europe.

Nevertheless, the upper mid-price fashion segment has also witnessed the rise of large brand collectors such as Phillips-Van Heusen, Iconix Brand Group and Liz Claiborne that are mostly located in the United States. Two of the most prominent recent deals conducted were the takeover of Tommy Hilfiger by Phillips-Van Heusen Corporation in March 2010 ($3.0bn) as well as the acquisition of outdoor footwear manufacturer The Timberland Company by VF Corporation in June 2011 for a consideration of $2.0bn. These mid-price fashion conglomerates also constitute multi-billion dollar businesses and have participated frequently in the takeover market to support their external growth strategy.

Still, the fashion industry exhibits a very heterogeneous business structure. While the above-mentioned conglomerates and some solid, stand-alone companies such as Polo Ralph Lauren and Hermès International are steadily increasing company sizes, there are also a great deal of small, single-brand businesses that are privately owned and closely associated with central personalities such as their founder or present creative director. Since many of these small businesses are attractive takeover candidates due to their company heritage and strong market awareness, future mergers and acquisitions are to be expected.

On the contrary, divestiture activities in the fashion industry are rather scarce and often related to either corporate refocusing programs or seller companies in situations of financial distress such as NexCen Brands and Tropical Sportswear. In Germany, the decline and subsequent bankruptcy of luxury ladies' fashion house ESCADA AG caught media attention during the first decade of the 21st century. ESCADA divested several of its non-core segments over the course of this period. In our clinical paper we concentrate on a particular divestiture process that heavily contributed to the company's demise.

Along with M&A activity, the fashion industry has also witnessed some high-profile initial public offerings in recent years. Prada's $2.1bn offering in June 2011 on the Hong Kong Stock Exchange was one of the largest fashion IPOs so far. With Tom Tailor Holding AG's 2010 offering, there was also a prominent German IPO during the preparation of this dissertation. The ongoing discussions about possible IPOs of Italian fashion houses Versace and Salvatore Ferragamo show that equity offerings are still an integral part of the fashion industry and appear as an attractive option for change of control processes.

Despite these enormous changes in industry structure and dynamics, there is only a very narrow literary base of corporate finance research on the fashion industry. One of the most prominent exceptions is the acclaimed case study on once highly successful US footwear manufacturer L.A. Gear's failure by DeAngelo et al. (2002). Königs and Schiereck (2008) further examine shareholder wealth effects for luxury goods M&A transactions which also include luxury fashion and leather accessories deals. This study, however, leaves out low- and mid-price fashion transactions and also considers non-fashion merger activity in segments such as jewelry, alcoholic beverages and wristwatches.

Bhattacharyya and Nain (2011) explicitly reference the apparel segment in their empirical study of horizontal mergers in various industries as an important example for strategic consolidation efforts in order to create high buying power towards suppliers. Finally, Mitchell and Mulherin (1996) investigate takeover and restructuring activity in different industries following exogenous shocks between 1982 and 1989. They confirm that consolidation in the apparel industry during this period was mainly driven by the emergence of foreign competitors and the reduction of trade barriers while giving a rather pessimistic outlook on M&A profitability for this particular time period. None of these studies, however, exclusively focuses on the apparel segment. Therefore, only little insights on long-term industry dynamics and value drivers are given.

To the best of our knowledge, a conclusive overview of corporate finance-related issues on the fashion and accessories industry has not yet been given. The research objective of this dissertation therefore is to shed a light on a variety of topics that revolve around the key factors of success of fashion companies. There are also undisputedly important aspects within the fields of marketing, sales, logistics and organization that determine corporate success in the fashion industry. For the sake of coherence and sharp focus, however, we dedicate this dissertation solely to matters of corporate finance and governance.

We divide our analysis into four central research questions. First, we take a look at short-term shareholder wealth effects that are generated by M&A deal announcements in the fashion and leather accessories industry. In a second step, we analyze the long-run operating performance of merging companies and their non-acquirer peers. Our third analysis concentrates on divestiture activities in the fashion industry with the help of a clinical paper on ESCADA's belated disposal of its non-core segment PRIMERA. Finally, we illustrate the long-term stock price performance of fashion initial public offerings and investigate shifts in the systematic risk exposure of apparel companies issuing equity.

In light of the ongoing consolidation in the fashion industry, we start our analysis with the following first research question: How do investors react to the announcement of an M&A transaction in the apparel industry? As an appropriate measure for shareholder wealth effects, we apply standard short-term event study methodology as outlined inter alia by Serra (2002), Binder (1998) and MacKinlay (1997). Since many target firms in our data sample are privately held companies with little or no publicly disclosed information, we rather concentrate on bidder stock price reactions. While most previous studies find highly positive and statistically significant abnormal returns to target shareholders, results for bidder companies vary across different industries and time periods.

Using a data set comprising 192 M&A transactions conducted between 1994 and 2009, we find positive and significant abnormal returns to bidding shareholders of fashion companies. Cross-sectional regression analysis reveals that wealth creation is highly positive especially for smaller bidding firms and first-time acquirers. Furthermore, there is a significantly negative correlation between abnormal returns and both acquirer market capitalization as well as multiple bids during the observation period. We therefore conclude that M&A deals conducted for the purpose of diversifying the high risk exposure of small, single-brand fashion companies are generally welcomed by equity investors.

On the other hand, the negative reaction to multiple bids and transactions of larger companies can most likely be attributed to arguments of the free cash flow (Jensen (1986)) and hubris hypotheses (Roll (1986)). These theories view M&A activity as a means to squander excess cash resources and to increase firm size as well as management reputation rather than corporate profitability. The same applies to transactions that have been conducted during bull markets with high cash availability as opposed to carefully-assessed strategic deals executed in times of economic downturn or even recessionary periods.

Having analyzed the announcement effects of fashion M&A transactions, we pose our second research question: How do these positive short-term reactions translate into more long-term oriented merger success? Generally, it would have been possible to evaluate long-run performance by using a buy-and-hold return event study as applied in studies such as Bouwman et al. (2009) and Agrawal et al. (1992). Due to a number of companies that conducted various deals, however, test results of a corresponding analysis would have been seriously biased due to the presence of many confounding events.

Instead, we measure long-term M&A success by comparing pre- and post-merger operating profitability, leverage and growth ratios for merging firms and their non-acquiring peer group companies. Following the methodology of Barber and Lyon (1996), we use several accounting ratios and a matched-firm approach to find abnormal operating performance. We use the same data sample as in our short-term event study, but have to eliminate 32 of the 192 original transactions due to the non-availability of sufficient accounting data.

Our analysis shows a significant drop in operating performance following the remaining 160 sample transactions compared to both pre-merger company financials as well as peer group firm performance. On the contrary, post-merger financial leverage significantly increases for merging companies. At first sight, this is not a surprising finding, since firms generally gain higher debt capacities following M&A activity due to larger company size, lower default risk and higher bargaining power in bank negotiations (Ghosh and Jain (2000)).

Nevertheless, cross-sectional regression analysis shows that post-merger debt ratios have a significantly negative influence on operating performance. We conclude that some merging companies have increased their leverage beyond the optimal point of indebtedness which puts additional distress on companies that are already engaged in costly post-merger integration activities. Finally, pre-merger cash availability and the general stock market climate again are negatively correlated to post-merger accounting performance. These findings give a mixed outlook on the general advantageousness of fashion M&A activity.

In case a company decides on a corporate restructuring or the anticipated synergies from an acquisition do not materialize, it might be beneficial to sell off parts of the business or a certain brand. Our third research question therefore is: What are the consequences of a divestiture in the fashion industry? Mostly due to the fact that our identified seller company data sample is rather small in order to draw reliable inferences from an empirical analysis, we illustrate the implications of divestiture activities by means of a clinical paper.

German luxury couture house ESCADA AG rose to international success and high reputation in the two decades following its foundation in 1976, reaching almost €1bn in annual sales volume at its peak. The company also supported its growth strategy by various mergers and acquisitions, joint ventures as well as licensing agreements in non-core segments such as affordable mid-price ladies' ready-to-wear fashion, kids wear, leather accessories, cosmetic products, sunglasses and jewelry, creating a widely-diversified brand portfolio.

As the company's profitability started to deteriorate at the end of the 1990s, management under founder Wolfgang Ley decided on a refocusing on ESCADA's core competencies in the luxury apparel segment. While most of the company's non-core activities were sold off subsequently, management adhered to PRIMERA AG, ESCADA's largest mid-price fashion segment that included four brands and accounted for roughly one quarter of the group's revenue in fiscal year 2000/2001. During the following decade, management insisted on its disposal plans for PRIMERA without initiating a divestiture process until the company finally faced serious financial distress at the end of 2008.

Since management itself proclaimed the lack of synergies between ESCADA's core business and the PRIMERA brands while independent broker reports at times consented on a very lucrative value range for the PRIMERA business of up to €200m, the prolonged disposal hesitation appears in stark contrast to the rational behavior hypothesis that is commonly cited in corporate finance research. Based on pertinent behavioral finance literature and publicly disclosed announcements of ESCADA management, we argue that psychological phenomena such as loss aversion, status quo bias and mental accounting exerted a tremendous influence on the reasonable decision to divest the subsidiary. In the absence of an efficient market for corporate control, management was able to delay the divestiture and thereby lead the company into bankruptcy.

Finally, we put forward our fourth and last research question: How do initial public offerings of fashion and leather accessories companies perform in the long-run and what are the key drivers of successful offerings? Numerous empirical studies such as Chang et al. (2010) and Brav and Gompers (1997) have analyzed long-term buy-and-hold returns and consistently found a significant underperformance of newly issued stocks compared to corresponding benchmarks across various industries, geographic regions and time periods.

Building on a data set comprising 207 fashion IPOs conducted between 1990 and 2007, we find that offerings are clustered during periods of high stock market valuations. In addition, IPO stocks experience an average price jump of 20.5% (commonly referred to as "money left on the table") from the offer price to the closing price at the end of the first trading week. Despite these very positive initial returns, issuing companies significantly underperform corresponding equity indices by up to 31.5% for a 36-month post-IPO holding period.

While long-term underperformance is often attributed to investor sentiment and asymmetrical information, we argue that there is a more rational explanation for the seemingly poor stock price development. We find that a large fraction of issuing companies intended to use their offer proceeds for investments in both internal and external growth opportunities. An analysis of pre- and post-IPO company financials confirms that capital expenditures as well as total assets and sales volumes significantly increase following fashion offerings.

We build our analysis on the theoretical model of Carlson et al. (2004) who argue that SEO companies use their offer proceeds to turn risky real options such as a potential M&A investment into lower-risk assets in place. When we analyze the development of post-IPO company betas, we find a considerable reduction of systematic risk. In the context of the risk-return spectrum, this confirms our hypothesis that the weak stock price performance of issuing companies is in large parts driven by a general risk reduction that is due to the realization of real options in company portfolios. This finding evokes a more optimistic outlook on IPO performance in the fashion business segment.

In summary, this dissertation gives a broad variety of insights into the dynamic environment of the fashion and leather accessories industry. We empirically investigate both short- and long-term implications of mergers and acquisitions, divestiture activities as well as initial public offerings in this business segment. On an academic level, we expand the existing corporate finance literature by novel findings on a specific, fast-growing industry that has been widely disregarded in previous scholarly works. Nevertheless, this dissertation also represents a helpful manual for various practitioners within financial institutions, venture capitalists and, not least, fashion and leather accessories companies. Based on our empirical findings, they should be able to draw significant inferences that will help them to understand the key drivers of success in the fashion industry and to make meaningful and sustainable strategic decisions.

2 SHORT-TERM WEALTH EFFECTS OF FASHION M&A TRANSACTIONS

2.1 INTRODUCTION

The fashion and leather accessories industry is an industry of already high market volumes and strong growth potentials, accounting for approximately $500bn in international trading volume (WTO (2010)). Like many other industries, the apparel segment is also in a state of ongoing consolidation. While a handful of fashion conglomerates have already built large and diversified brand portfolios in recent years, there are still many small, privately held mono-brand apparel companies left that appeal as attractive takeover targets to potential bidders.

Despite the industry's volume and growth potential, the apparel segment is also a cyclical business and bears a serious idiosyncratic risk. Previous research such as the case study of DeAngelo et al. (2002) that focuses on the collapse of the athletic footwear company L.A. Gear show the need for clothing firms to quickly adapt to current trends in a competitive and fast-paced environment. A once-missed trend can especially endanger the survival of smaller, mono-structured companies. It is remarkable that until now, little research activity has been conducted that focuses on this specific market segment.

The objective of this paper is to analyze the value implications of mergers and acquisitions in the fashion and accessories industry and to determine the market dynamics of this segment from 1994 to 2009. We conduct an event study analyzing the short-term shareholder wealth effects of 192 global M&A transaction announcements on bidder stock prices. The examination of univariate subsamples further differentiates between various types of deals such as luxury and mid-price level fashion transactions as well as domestic and cross-border deals. Finally, we apply cross-sectional regression analysis to identify key value drivers in fashion M&A deals and examine the specific differences in announcement effects to acquiring shareholders.

The paper proceeds as follows. Section 2.2 sheds a light on the (narrow) literary base of existing corporate finance research on the fashion and accessories sector as well as the framework and previous applications of the event study methodology. Section 2.3 illustrates our selection criteria for the definition of the data sample and explains the methodology applied in this paper. Detailed descriptive statistics of acquiring and target companies' financials, geographic and seasonal distributions are also given. Section 2.4 presents the results of our short-term event study as well as the cross-sectional regression analysis. Section 2.5 summarizes our findings and concludes.

2.2 LITERATURE OVERVIEW

The event study methodology which was introduced in a seminal paper by Fama et al. (1969) is today the central instrument in event-driven corporate valuation research. It is based on capital market perceptions of value. Under the assumptions of efficient capital markets as defined by Fama (1970), a firm's stock price is supposed to reflect the unbiased value of discounted future cash flows. Consequently, stock prices are assumed to correctly and instantly incorporate all (publicly) available information about the firm.

Kothari and Warner (2007) give an overview of the broad literary base and identify a total of 565 conducted event studies (no surveys and theoretical papers) in the five leading financial journals in the period from 1974 to 2000 alone. In a majority of these papers such as Goergen and Renneboog (2004), DeLong (2001), Jarrell and Poulsen (1989) and Langestieg (1978), target shareholders are reported to gain high and statistically significant, positive cumulative abnormal returns (CAR) upon the announcement of M&A transactions.

Stock price reactions to M&A announcements for acquiring shareholders, however, do not follow a consistent pattern throughout previous research. While Mulherin and Boone (2000) and Asquith et al. (1983) find significant positive CAR for bidder companies, others such as Franks et al. (1991) report insignificant results that range close around zero. In some research, e.g. by Moeller et al. (2005), Kaplan and Weisbach (1992) and Malestata (1983), acquiring shareholders even suffer significantly negative cumulative abnormal returns.

These mostly skeptical stock market reactions are often attributed to arguments of M&A as a form of wasteful investment and managerial overconfidence. The free cash flow hypothesis by Jensen (1986) argues that corporate managers would rather invest into NPV-negative projects then pay out excess cash resources accumulated in times of high free cash flow generation as dividends to shareholders. The hubris theory by Roll (1986) further assumes that M&A activity is mostly conducted to increase company sizes and thereby management reputation ("empire-building"). Both hypotheses underline the assumption that M&A transactions are value-destructive to bidding shareholders.

In addition to general event studies that include companies from multiple lines of business and geographical regions, a large body of research focuses entirely on certain country- or industry-specific M&A transactions. Event studies with acquiring and/or target firms from one particular geographical area were conducted e.g. for the (US-)American (Wansley et al. (1983)), British (Firth (1980)), Canadian (Eckbo and Thorburn (2000)), European (Campa and Hernando (2004)) and German markets (Boehmer and Löffler (1999)).

In terms of industry-specific research, Mentz and Schiereck (2008) investigate shareholder wealth effects in the automotive industry while Beitel et al. (2004) and Houston et al. (2001) concentrate on the implications of bank mergers. Clement et al. (2007) analyze wealth effects of new movie releases to producing companies, Berry (2000) focuses on transactions in the electric utility segment and Ahnefeld et al. (2006) survey consolidation in the water industry.

To the best of our knowledge, an event study focusing on the fashion industry with its specific idiosyncratic risk characteristics, high upfront costs of developing new collections at least twice per year and, in larger corporations, a huge amount of regularly generated free cash flows has not yet been conducted. While Königs and Schiereck (2008) survey the luxury goods sector and also cover luxury fashion and accessories transactions, they leave out the lower and mid-price fashion segment. It will therefore be of great interest to determine the differences in market dynamics between these two segments.

While the fashion industry has seen an enormous degree of consolidation over the previous decades, even large conglomerates such as LVMH, Phillips-Van Heusen Corporation and Iconix Brand Group have barely participated in cross-continental M&A transactions and rather focused on target companies in their home and adjacent countries. Aggarwal and Kyaw (2010) associate multinationality with lower debt ratios and higher dividend payments. Kim and Mathur (2008) as well as Olibe et al. (2008) report a decrease in firm value and higher systematic risk associated with geographical diversification, respectively. In light of these considerations, we also analyze the differences in shareholder value creation between domestic and cross-border transactions.

As an additionally surprising finding, there have been only very few large M&A transactions in the fashion and leather accessories industry. The takeover of Reebok by Adidas (2005, $4.2bn) as well as French luxury conglomerate PPR SA's acquisitions of both Gucci Group (2001, >$8bn) and Puma (2007, $4.4bn) were the only deals that exceeded $1bn in purchase prices during the first decade of the 21st century. We therefore conduct both univariate as well as cross-sectional regression analyses to find out as to what extent deal size affects shareholder wealth generation in fashion M&A transactions.

2.3 DATA AND METHODOLOGY

2.3.1 Data

We identify bidder M&A transactions in the fashion and leather accessories industry using the SDC/Thomson One Banker Deals database. To determine relevant acquirer companies, the World Luxury Index by Deutsche Boerse AG and BNP Paribas as well as the MSCI Textiles, Apparel, and Luxury Goods sector index were used. In addition, broker reports by miscellaneous investment banks' research divisions on the fashion and accessories as well as the luxury goods industry were screened for relevant public companies.[1]

Since this event study is focused solely on fashion and leather accessories M&A transactions, we further exclude all companies that specialize in closely associated non-fashion industry segments such as the production and distribution of eyewear (e.g. Luxottica, Safilo and De Rigo), wristwatches (e.g. Swatch Group) and jewelry (e.g. Bulgari, Damiani Group and Tiffany & Co.).

Since missing companies that were acquired, delisted or that declared bankruptcy during the observation period could bias the sample, we conduct research for all M&A deals involving bidder companies with the primary two-digit SIC codes in the major groups "23 – Apparel and Other Finished Products Made From Fabrics And Similar Materials" and "56 – Apparel and Accessory Stores". Due to potential misspecifications, we verify the correctness of SIC codes using internet research on the respective companies (Kahle and Walkling (1996)).

The initial sample comprises 81 relevant public acquirer companies from 14 countries that were involved in 1,191 mergers and acquisitions during the period from 1 January 1994 to 31 December 2009. We then use the following filter criteria to further select relevant M&A transactions:

(1) Both the acquirer and target company operate in the fashion and leather accessories industry as defined by their primary two-digit SIC code.

(2) The bidder company is a publicly listed entity and liquid daily trading data for 273 trading days preceding and 20 trading days following the event date is available on Thomson Financial Datastream.

---

[1] Sector coverages by the following investment banks were screened: Bank of America Merrill Lynch, Barclays Capital, Berenberg Bank, Citibank, Deutsche Bank, Lazard Capital Markets, Leonardo & Co., Morgan Stanley, Nomura, The Royal Bank of Scotland, UBS and Woori Investment & Securities.

(3) The status of the transaction is denominated “completed”.

(4) A controlling stake (>50% of voting shares) has been acquired.

Criterion (1) is applied to rule out financial investments and private equity transactions and to account only for strategic acquisitions. For the purpose of conducting an event study, the acquirer has to be listed on a stock exchange and liquid trading data for the event window and estimation period has to be available, hence criterion (2). By applying criterion (3), transactions that were withdrawn or only rumored about are excluded. In case a transaction status was denominated “pending” in the SDC database, we conduct internet research to verify whether the transaction has been completed in the meantime.

Since transaction values have only been available for roughly 70% of relevant M&A transactions, a minimum deal value as is commonly applied in similar event studies is not mandatory for data sample inclusion. Drees et al. (2011) and Poulsen (2011) find that minority block purchases and toehold acquisitions have significantly different value implications than majority stake acquisitions with change of control consequences. Therefore, criterion (4) determines that deals are only included if a controlling stake is acquired.

In case a fashion company acquires another firm in multiple transaction steps (e.g. in LVMH’s takeover of Italian fashion house Fendi), we only consider the transaction in which the controlling stake is acquired. If one company acquired two or more targets on the same day, all of these transactions were excluded from the data sample since the resulting cumulative abnormal returns cannot be attributed to a specific transaction using the event study methodology.

To control for a possible bias due to the occurrence of confounding events, all transactions that were executed by a company within the event window of another transaction by the same firm are marked and checked for the robustness of test results using two data samples including and excluding these follow-up transactions. We find that these transactions do not qualitatively affect our test results and therefore maintain these deals within our data sample.

After all criteria are applied to the initial sample, a total of 192 bidder transactions with a grand total of disclosed deal values in the amount of $25,480.85m are remaining. Deal values have been disclosed for 131 deals, implying an average transaction value of $194.51m. Of the originally identified 81 companies, 55 bidders from 12 countries were involved in at least one transaction for which daily trading data is available. A detailed overview of the distribution of transactions among the involved bidders is illustrated in table 2.1.

Table 2.1: Number and volumes of fashion M&A deals per company

ACQUIRER NAME	NO.	VOLUME (IN $M)	ACQUIRER NAME	NO.	VOLUME (IN $M)
Active Apparel Group Inc	1	60.00	Kenneth Cole Productions	1	25.00
adidas AG	5	4,293.88	Lambert Howarth Group PLC	1	33.28
Ahlers AG	6	69.45	Liz Claiborne Inc	11	1,042.27
BasicNet SpA	2	41.06	LVMH Moet-Hennessy SA	12	1,626.12
Benetton Group SpA	4	378.31	Mariella Burani SpA	10	171.79
Billabong International Ltd	5	131.62	Marzotto SpA	2	221.33
Calida AG	1	0.00	NexCen Brands Inc	1	70.80
Charles Voegele Holding AG	1	49.75	Nike Inc.	5	1,320.29
Charming Shoppes Inc	1	334.98	Nordstrom Inc	1	163.00
Christian Dior SA	1	346.29	Oxford Industries Inc	1	0.00
Coach Inc	1	300.00	Perry Ellis International Inc	6	308.45
Columbia Sportswear Co	4	79.40	Phillips-Van Heusen Corp	7	1,192.50
Compagnie Financière Richemont	2	13.10	Polo Ralph Lauren	8	1,182.90
EganaGoldpfeil Holdings Ltd.	5	72.44	PPR SA	2	5,303.75
Escada AG	1	0.00	PUMA AG	3	38.62
Esprit Holdings Ltd	5	912.90	Quiksilver Inc	5	304.53
Foot Locker Inc	2	327.00	Sara Lee Corp	1	0.00
Gap Inc	1	150.00	Sirena Apparel Group Inc	1	0.00
Gildan Activewear Inc	2	180.50	Sport-Haley Inc.	1	0.17
Gucci Group NV	7	259.10	Tarrant Apparel Group	1	0.00
Guess Inc.	2	22.57	Timberland Co	3	82.00
H&M Hennes & Mauritz AB	2	92.24	Tommy Hilfiger USA Inc	2	1,528.81
Hartmarx Corp	2	0.00	VF Corp	16	1,434.72
Hermes International SCA	3	0.00	Warnaco Group Inc	2	325.81
Hugo Boss AG	2	0.00	Wolford AG	1	0.00
Iconix Brand Group Inc	10	668.90	Wolverine World Wide Inc	7	46.25
Industria de Diseno Textil SA	1	50.22	Wünsche AG	1	83.97
IT Holding SpA	1	140.78	**TOTAL**	**192**	**25,480.85**

The majority of fashion and leather accessories M&A deals (104 out of 192) were executed by bidder companies from the United States of America. With a total of 62 transactions from acquirer companies headquartered in Germany, Italy and France, the big European fashion and accessories markets represent another large proportion of the remaining takeovers. Table 2.2 shows the geographical distribution of bidding companies per country as well as the respective number of deals and corresponding disclosed transaction values.

Table 2.3 shows some of the most important acquirer company financials and key ratios that are also used in the cross-sectional regression analysis. All balance sheet items shown in this table are taken from the end of the fiscal year preceding the transaction announcement. The data show a concentration of mostly medium-sized businesses with rather solid earnings situations.

Table 2.2: Geographical distribution of fashion M&A deals

ACQUIRER NATION	NUMBER OF COMPANIES	PERCEN-TAGE	NUMBER OF DEALS	PERCEN-TAGE	VOLUME (IN $M)
USA	28	50.9%	104	54.2%	10,970.34
Germany	6	10.9%	18	9.4%	4,485.92
Italy	6	10.9%	26	13.5%	1,212.37
France	4	7.3%	18	9.4%	7,276.17
Switzerland	3	5.5%	4	2.1%	62.86
Hong Kong	2	3.6%	10	5.2%	985.34
Canada	1	1.8%	2	1.0%	180.50
Australia	1	1.8%	5	2.6%	131.62
Sweden	1	1.8%	2	1.0%	92.24
Spain	1	1.8%	1	0.5%	50.22
United Kingdom	1	1.8%	1	0.5%	33.28
Austria	1	1.8%	1	0.5%	0.00
TOTAL	**55**	**100.0%**	**192**	**100.0%**	**25,480.85**

Skewness measures for some of the financials and ratios illustrated in table 2.3 imply a lack of normality in the distribution. This is especially noticeable for the size measures such as market capitalization, sales volume and total assets that are considerably skewed right. The return on equity distribution, however, is significantly skewed left due to a handful of strongly negative outliers such as then minimum of -105.79% that accounts to German Wünsche AG's serious net loss in fiscal year 1997 preceding its 1998 acquisition of Joop! GmbH. Means for cash to total assets and free cash flows are considerable, implying a strong potential for cash generation by fashion and leather accessories companies.

Table 2.3: Key financials and ratios of acquiring companies

COMPANY FINANCIALS	MEAN	MEDIAN	MIN	MAX	SKEWNESS	STANDARD DEVIATION
Market capitalization (in $m)	5,325.12	1,957.35	16.56	52,250.08	2.82	8,804.16
Sales (in $m)	3,446.46	1,516.29	10.37	25,053.31	2.39	4,621.51
EBIT (in $m)	464.56	182.72	-55.75	4,700.23	2.84	678.86
Total assets (in $m)	3,858.66	1,276.77	8.27	42,052.10	3.27	6,547.21
Cash to total assets (in %)	14.88%	11.05%	0.31%	58.62%	1.38	12.71%
Debt ratio (in %)	27.41%	23.36%	0.00%	85.23%	0.77	19.29%
Market-to-book ratio (x)	2.66x	2.35x	0.50x	10.28x	1.80	1.59x
Return on equity (in %)	14.15%	15.22%	-105.79%	51.63%	-5.43	14.41%
Free cash flow (in $m)	367.07	133.17	-46.67	3,095.44	2.50	528.27

In our sample transactions, target companies from 23 countries and five continents were acquired (see table 2.4). The majority of deals were domestic transactions (57.3%), cross-border transactions within the same continent account for 17.7% and the remaining 25.0% are cross-continental M&A deals. The single most common deal type were transactions involving both acquirer and target companies from the United States (39.1%), followed by all-Italian domestic deals (9.4%). The predominance of US American companies might well be explained with a clustering of mid-price fashion businesses (the luxury fashion companies such as LVMH, PPR and Hermès are mostly located in Europe) as well as a larger percentage of publicly listed companies in the USA.

Table 2.4: Geographical distributions of bidder and target companies[2]

TARGET NATION

ACQUIRER NATION	AT	AU	BR	CA	CH	CN	DE	ES	FR	GB	HK	IE	IN	IT	JP	LT	NL	PT	RU	SE	TR	US	UY	TOTAL
AT	1																							1
AU		2																				3		5
BR																								0
CA																						2		2
CH									2		1						1							4
CN																								0
DE			1	1	2		7		1								1			1		4		18
ES																			1					1
FR						1	1	1	4	1		1	1	6			1					1		18
GB										1														1
HK	1				1	1	5				1											1		10
IE																								0
IN																								0
IT	1		1		1		1		1	1				18		1					1			26
JP																								0
LT																								0
NL																								0
PT																								0
RU																								0
SE							1													1				2
TR																								0
US		1		5		1	1		3	5			1	6	2		2	1				75	1	104
UY																								0
TOTAL	3	3	2	6	4	3	16	1	11	8	2	1	2	30	2	1	5	1	1	2	1	86	1	192

The distribution of deals per year during the observation period shows a large concentration during years of economic upswing and favorable stock market climates. The single most deals were executed in 2006 (10.9%), followed by

2 AT=Austria, AU=Australia, BR=Brazil, CA=Canada, CH=Switzerland, CN=China, DE= Germany, ES=Spain, FR=France, GB=United Kingdom, HK=Hong Kong, IE=Republic of Ireland, IN=India, IT=Italy, JP=Japan, LT=Lithuania, NL=Netherlands, PT=Portugal, RU=Russian Federation, SE=Sweden, TR=Turkey, US=United States, UY=Uruguay

2005 and 2007 (both 9.4%). On the contrary, the last two years of the observation period show a significant downward effect that was most likely caused by the financial crisis. We will therefore determine the influence that the overall stock market performance exerts on the magnitude of wealth generation by M&A in our cross-sectional regression analysis. We assume that crisis deals have significantly different value implications for bidder companies than transactions that were executed during boom phases with high stock market valuation levels. Table 2.5 illustrates the distribution of deals per year.

Table 2.5: Distributions of fashion M&A transactions per year

YEAR	NUMBER OF TRANSACTIONS	PERCENTAGE	CUMULATIVE PERCENTAGE	DEAL VOLUME (IN $M)
1994	3	1.6%	1.6%	854.97
1995	6	3.1%	4.7%	707.53
1996	8	4.2%	8.9%	286.07
1997	7	3.6%	12.5%	342.62
1998	7	3.6%	16.1%	1,416.96
1999	14	7.3%	23.4%	984.67
2000	17	8.9%	32.3%	735.83
2001	14	7.3%	39.6%	2,216.98
2002	10	5.2%	44.8%	1,450.68
2003	14	7.3%	52.1%	1,291.77
2004	16	8.3%	60.4%	1,250.56
2005	18	9.4%	69.8%	5,391.13
2006	21	10.9%	80.7%	1,119.19
2007	18	9.4%	90.1%	5,989.85
2008	10	5.2%	95.3%	652.12
2009	9	4.7%	100.0%	789.94
TOTAL	**192**	**100.0%**	**100.0%**	**25,480.85**

2.3.2 Methodology

As a measure of value creation in fashion M&A transactions, standard event study methodology is used. We retrieve daily stock returns for all sample companies that were adjusted for dividend payments and changes to the capital structure (R_{jt}) and the returns on the corresponding benchmark indices (R_{bt}) from Thomson Financial Datastream. The market model is used as an estimator for abnormal stock price performance (Brown and Warner (1980, 1985)):

$$(1)\quad E(R_{jt}) = \alpha_j + \beta_j * R_{bt} + \varepsilon_{jt}$$

where $E(R_{jt})$ is the expected return of company *j*'s stock on day *t*, α_j and β_j are the model parameters that are estimated using the OLS regression during the estimation period, R_{bt} is the return on the benchmark index *b* on day *t* and ε_{jt} is the residual disturbance term. Abnormal returns of company j's stock on day t (AR_{jt}) are calculated by subtracting the expected stock returns ($E(R_{jt})$) from the actual stock returns (R_{jt}) in the event window:

(2) $AR_{jt} = R_{jt} - E(R_{jt})$

For the estimation period, we observe a time series of one full trading year (252 trading days) preceding the event window. The event window has a length of 41 trading days, starting twenty days before and ending twenty days after the announcement day (see figure 2.1). Abnormal returns for each day of the event window are then added up to calculate cumulative abnormal returns:

(3) $CAR_{j[t1;\, t2]} = \sum_{t_1}^{t_2} AR_{jt}$

with:

CAR_j = Cumulative abnormal return for company j

$[t_1; t_2]$ = Event window ranging from days t_1 to t_2

Figure 2.1: Event study estimation period and event window lengths

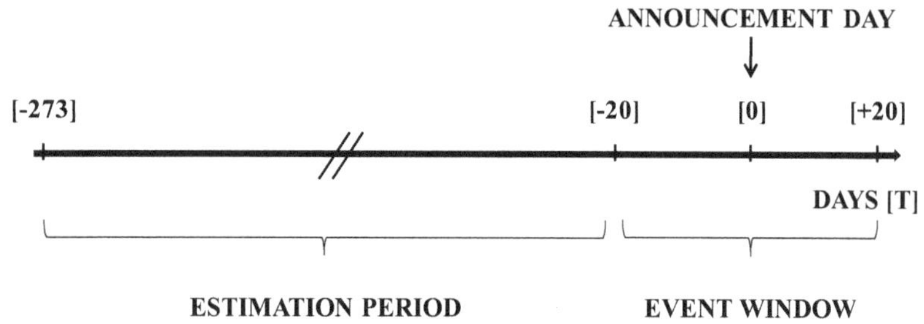

We use the parametric test statistic of Boehmer et al. (1991) to test for the statistical significance of the cumulative average abnormal returns (CAAR) of the data sample (Harrington and Shrider (2007)). Standard t-test statistics as well as a constant mean model are applied to check our results for coherence. We also use a non-parametric Wilcoxon signed-rank test for the statistical significance of medians. The same approach is applied to a number of univariate sub-samples that differentiate between luxury and mid-price fashion segment deals, domestic and cross-border transactions as well as three different deal size categories.

In order to identify the key value drivers of fashion and leather accessories M&A transactions, we apply cross-sectional regression analysis to a series of acquirer- and transaction-specific deal characteristics. We use the cumulative abnormal return of each transaction for the [-1; +1] event window as the dependent variable. As for the independent variables, a series of acquirer- and transaction-specific criteria is applied. In this context, the criteria "luxury transaction", "cross-border transaction" and "100% cash payment" are binary dummy variables that take on the value 1 in case the criterion is fulfilled by the respective transaction and the value 0 if not.

The criteria "1st bid" and "5th bid or higher" are also binary variables (Fuller et al. (2002)). "1st bid" takes on the value 1 if the transaction is the first to be executed by a particular company within the time period from 1994 to 2009. "5th bid or higher", on the other hand, takes on the value 1 in case a company has completed at least four other fashion M&A deals during the respective time window preceding the transaction under consideration. We use these two criteria to analyze the wealth effects to both shareholders of companies that make only few selected acquisitions as well as firms with high takeover frequencies.

The cyclicality of M&A deals is measured using the rebased price/earnings ratio of the Datastream World Clothing & Accessories index as an indicator of the overall valuation level of stock markets (Erxleben and Schiereck (2010)). Bidding company financials include acquirer market capitalization, cash to total assets, debt ratio (total book value of debt to total assets), market-to-book ratio and return on equity that were all retrieved from Thomson Financial Datastream. Deal size and method of payment were derived from the SDC/Thomson One Banker Deals database. Relative transaction size is defined as deal value divided by the acquiring company's market capitalization on the announcement day.

We use the heteroscedasticity-consistent test procedure by White (1980) with adjusted standard errors as our main test statistic. As a check for robustness, a standard OLS regression model is also used. To check for the presence of autocorrelation, we apply the test procedure of Durbin and Watson (1950, 1951).

2.4 RESULTS

Table 2.6 illustrates the key results of our analysis of short-term wealth effects. We find highly significant, positive cumulative abnormal returns. This positive capital market perception stands in opposite compared to a large fraction of previous cross-industry research on wealth effects for acquiring shareholders. M&A transactions in the fashion and leather accessories industry therefore generate shareholder value for both target and bidder companies.

Table 2.6: Event study results for fashion M&A data sample transactions

EVENT WINDOW	CUMULATIVE ABNORMAL RETURN		T-TEST	BOEHMER-TEST	WILCOXON SIGNED-RANK TEST
Days (t)	Mean	Median	t-value	z-score	z-score
[-20;+20]	1.71%	0.90%	1.589	1.501	-1.096
[-10;+10]	2.01%	1.05%	2.611***	2.635***	-2.149**
[-5;+5]	1.30%	0.54%	2.280**	2.355**	-1.569
[-1;+1]	1.16%	0.56%	3.291***	3.321***	-2.883***
[0;+0]	0.79%	0.15%	3.059***	3.198***	-2.086**
[0;+1]	1.11%	0.45%	3.361***	3.454***	-3.203***
[0;+5]	1.26%	0.32%	2.646***	2.802***	-1.772*
[0;+10]	1.37%	0.33%	2.552**	2.625***	-1.843*
[0;+20]	1.39%	1.31%	1.791*	1.796*	-1.392

***, **, and * indicate statistical significance at the 1%, 5%, and 10% levels, respectively.

Figure 2.2 further illustrates the cumulative average abnormal returns for every single day of the [-20; +20] event window for the 192 bidder companies as well as the nine M&A transactions in which the target company was also a listed entity and liquid daily trading data was available for the estimation period and event window on Thomson Financial Datastream.

Figure 2.2: Bidder and target CAAR for the [-20; +20] event window

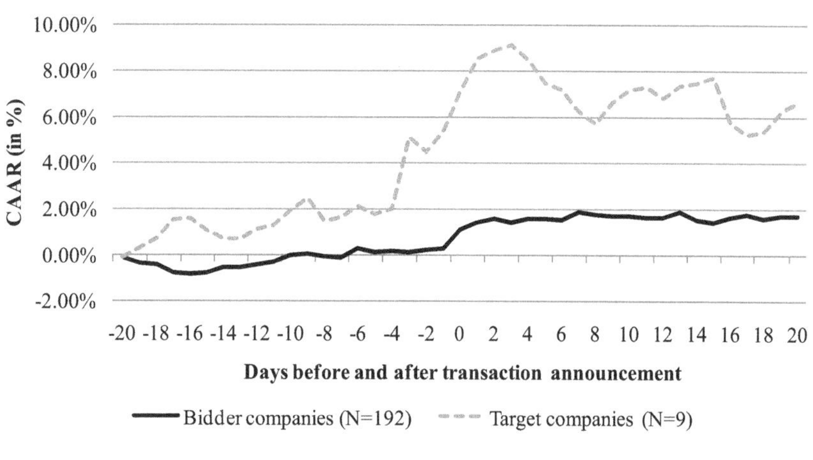

We further split our data sample into seven categories in which we investigate the wealth effects for three different kinds of univariate sub-samples. Categories 1 and 2 first differentiate between luxury and mid-price fashion segment M&A transactions. The classification of "luxury" transactions in this context is a subjective estimation that is based on a particular company's inclusion in various luxury indices as illustrated in section 2.3.1. Throughout all sub-samples illustrated in this chapter, the classifications ***, **, and * indicate statistical significance at the 1%, 5% and 10% levels, respectively. We also run two-sample t-test statistics in order to test differences in short-term announcement effects between different sub-samples for statistical significance.

In our first sub-sample (see table 2.7), standard fashion deals account for strongly significant, positive value implications whereas luxury fashion M&A transactions are significant only in the three event windows that immediately surround the announcement day. While differences in CAR are not statistically significant based on a two-sample t-test, we nevertheless get a first indication for a possible source of value creation in fashion and accessories M&A deals which seem to be driven especially by affordable ready-to-wear fashion.

Table 2.7: Luxury and standard fashion M&A sub-samples

	LUXURY DEALS (N=71)			STANDARD DEALS (N=121)			
Event window	**CAR**	**Boehmer**	**Wilcoxon**	**CAR**	**Boehmer**	**Wilcoxon**	**Two-sample t-Test**
Days (t)	Mean	z-score	z-score	Mean	z-score	z-score	t-value
[-20;+20]	-0.22%	-0.050	-0.546	2.76%	1.846*	-1.742*	-1.332
[-10;+10]	0.42%	0.598	-0.154	2.87%	2.784***	-2.456**	-1.533
[-5;+5]	0.42%	0.808	-0.199	1.79%	2.287**	-1.880*	-1.141
[-1;+1]	1.21%	2.353**	-2.192**	1.14%	2.384**	-2.071**	0.106
[0;+0]	0.64%	2.305**	-1.657*	0.87%	2.399**	-1.360	-0.424
[0;+1]	1.48%	3.156***	-2.996***	0.91%	2.047**	-1.811*	0.829
[0;+5]	0.39%	0.785	-0.206	1.74%	2.822***	-2.270**	-1.352
[0;+10]	0.13%	0.252	-0.395	2.05%	2.953***	-2.479**	-1.722
[0;+20]	1.65%	1.398	-0.879	1.26%	1.221	-0.971	0.238

Table 2.8 further illustrates the differences between domestic and cross-border transactions. As pointed out earlier, for the major part of deals the respective acquirer and target companies are headquartered in the same country. Of the 82 foreign transactions, 34 are intra-continental deals whereas 48 are cross-continental in nature. Looking at the results for these sub-samples, we derive a further indication for value drivers in fashion M&A deals. While cumulative abnormal returns are highly significant and substantial for domestic transactions, cross-border deals only earn small, hardly significant CAR throughout the entire observation period. Again, these differences in wealth creation are not significant using the two-sample t-test statistic.

Table 2.8: Domestic and cross-border M&A sub-samples

	DOMESTIC M&A (N=110)			CROSS-BORDER M&A (N=82)			
Event window	CAR	Boehmer	Wilcoxon	CAR	Boehmer	Wilcoxon	Two-sample t-Test
Days (t)	Mean	z-score	z-score	Mean	z-score	z-score	t-value
[-20;+20]	3.57%	2.074**	-2.076**	-0.69%	-0.281	-0.782	0.832
[-10;+10]	3.30%	2.823***	-2.540**	0.31%	0.609	-0.101	1.022
[-5;+5]	1.86%	2.034**	-1.550	0.61%	1.215	-0.633	0.470
[-1;+1]	1.63%	3.019***	-2.592***	0.58%	1.514	-1.501	0.717
[0;+0]	0.94%	2.548**	-1.793*	0.60%	1.907*	-1.127	-0.439
[0;+1]	1.27%	2.601***	-2.408**	0.91%	2.264**	-2.101**	-0.321
[0;+5]	1.45%	2.206**	-1.543	1.04%	1.728*	-0.897	-0.364
[0;+10]	1.88%	2.581***	-2.004**	0.72%	0.972	-0.302	0.491
[0;+20]	2.20%	2.097**	-1.773*	0.40%	0.321	-0.048	0.286

The third sub-sample illustrates the value creation of different deal size categories. The nine large value transactions with a purchase price of more than $500m induce CAR of almost 5% for the [-1; +1] and [0; +1] windows and are significant at the 1% level. Medium-sized transactions with a deal value of between $50m and $500m as well as small M&A deals with considerations of less than $50m also create significantly positive wealth effects for bidding shareholders. However, the CAR of these transactions are less ostentatious compared to the abnormal returns of the large deal value sub-sample. These results imply that large transactions in the fashion and leather accessories industry are indeed quite rare, but they do not support the suspicion that these deals are value-destructive as suggested e.g. by Moeller et al. (2005).

Table 2.9: Small, medium and large M&A deal size sub-samples

	VALUE > $500M (N=9)			VALUE < $500M (N=63)			VALUE < $50M (N=59)		
Event window	CAR	Boehmer	Wilcoxon	CAR	Boehmer	Wilcoxon	CAR	Boehmer	Wilcoxon
Days (t)	Mean	z-score	z-score	Mean	z-score	z-score	Mean	z-score	z-score
[-20;+20]	4.79%	0.705	0.793	3.56%	1.701*	-1.752*	1.37%	0.854	-0.662
[-10;+10]	3.33%	0.711	0.722	3.23%	2.260**	-2.039**	2.27%	2.075**	-1.659*
[-5;+5]	4.89%	1.453	1.327	2.53%	2.428**	-2.267**	0.63%	0.874	-0.687
[-1;+1]	4.94%	2.599***	2.333**	1.43%	1.990**	-2.032**	1.56%	2.446**	-2.153**
[0;+0]	1.61%	1.810*	1.545	1.35%	2.359**	-2.488**	0.74%	1.900*	-0.561
[0;+1]	4.57%	2.775***	2.488**	1.39%	1.997**	-2.400**	1.21%	2.056**	-1.542
[0;+5]	3.65%	1.337	1.324	1.48%	1.631	-1.090	1.25%	1.815*	-1.391
[0;+10]	2.04%	0.465	0.613	1.11%	1.005	-0.795	2.70%	2.842***	-2.187**
[0;+20]	3.14%	0.586	0.825	1.28%	0.710	-0.677	2.23%	1.846*	-1.290

Having described the value effects of M&A transactions, we apply cross-sectional analyses to identify the drivers of this value generation. We design five models to control for the validity of the different explanatory variables. Models M1 and M2 take into account all 192 transactions whereas models M3 and M4 only consider the 131 transactions for which deal values were disclosed in the SDC database. Model M5 contains 71 deals that were classified as luxury transactions. Table 2.10 reports the results of our cross-sectional analysis.

In model M1, the dummy variable "5th bid or higher" and the logarithm of the acquirer market capitalization are both negative and statistically significant. This implies a negative correlation between acquirer size as well as high takeover frequency and the corresponding stock price performance following M&A announcements in the fashion industry. Due to the existence of multicollinearity we eliminate the "5th bid or higher" dummy in model M2 which results in the binary variable "1st bid" becoming statistically significant and positive.

We interpret this finding as an indicator that selected acquisitions are favorable since they allow especially smaller firms to reduce a portion of their risk exposure. If a company only owns a single fashion brand, its idiosyncratic risk is very high due to the uncertainty of customer appreciation of a particular season's fashion collection. In case a collection does not meet customer demands, a large portion of the firm's sales is gravely endangered. Angelidis and Andrikopoulos (2010) show how idiosyncratic risk factors influence stock returns. The acquisition of a second brand would therefore help to diversify the company's risk exposure and is positively evaluated by the bidding shareholders.

Our results also imply that excessive takeover activity does not infinitely increase firm performance. There seems to be a trade-off between the benefits of risk diversification by making few selected acquisitions on one hand and the decreasing improvement opportunities that come along with executing numerous M&A deals on the other. This is confirmed by the fact that the "5th bid or higher" dummy remains negative and significant throughout models M3 to M5. The logarithm of the market value is also significantly negative in models M2, M3 and M4 which additionally underlines our central finding.

We therefore conclude that fashion and accessories companies need to cautiously evaluate their M&A decisions to successfully balance the opportunities for the reduction of their idiosyncratic risk exposure and the risk of conducting wasteful investments that come along with making random, complexity-increasing acquisitions that are binding integration capacities and do not enhance firm performance or create synergy effects on a net basis.

Table 2.10: Results of cross-sectional regression analysis

MODEL	M1	M2	M3	M4	M5
INTERCEPT	**0.0650****	**0.0624****	**0.0894****	**0.1047*****	**0.0978*****
	(2.2975)	(2.1049)	(2.2765)	(2.8033)	(3.5365)
DUMMY VARIABLES					
Luxury transaction	0.0062	0.0059	0.0045	0.0047	
	(0.8912)	(0.8243)	(0.4979)	(0.5176)	
Cross-border transaction	-0.0061	-0.0041	0.0003	-0.0026	-0.0074
	-(0.9930)	-(0.6821)	(0.0361)	-(0.3546)	-(0.8037)
1st bid	0.0053	**0.0127***			
	(0.6824)	(1.8210)			
5th bid or higher	**-0.02111*****		**-0.0193****	**-0.0205****	**-0.0236****
	-(2.6775)		-(2.1554)	-(2.2269)	-(2.5914)
DEAL CHARACTERISTICS					
Deal value			0.0000	**0.0000****	
			(1.1506)	(2.0512)	
Relative transaction size			0.0332		
			(1.1558)		
100% cash payment			-0.0103	-0.0124	
			-(1.2706)	-(1.5007)	
ACQUIRER FINANCIALS					
Log market cap	**-0.0133****	**-0.0168*****	**-0.0186****	**-0.0234*****	-0.0010
	-(2.2846)	-(2.8265)	-(2.1994)	-(2.9855)	-(0.1586)
Cash to total assets	-0.0135	-0.0064	-0.0351	-0.0312	-0.0496
	-(0.3974)	-(0.1954)	-(0.6220)	-(0.5615)	-(1.4073)
Debt ratio	-0.0133	-0.0162	-0.0323	-0.0261	-0.0275
	-(0.5131)	-(0.6296)	-(0.9949)	-(0.7856)	-(1.0271)
Market-to-book ratio	0.0011	0.0013	**0.0043****	**0.0043***	0.0010
	(0.4823)	(0.5788)	(2.0094)	(1.9687)	(0.4648)
Return on equity	0.0292	**0.0341***	**0.0424****	**0.0417****	**0.0344****
	(1.4806)	(1.8334)	(2.1683)	(2.0677)	(2.4507)
CYCLICALITY					
DS World Clothing P/E ratio	-0.0003	-0.0002	-0.0006	-0.0004	**-0.0026*****
	-(0.5525)	-(0.3240)	-(0.6819)	-(0.4965)	-(2.9406)
N	192	192	131	131	71
Adj. R^2	0.0745	0.0433	0.0846	0.0732	0.1592
F-statistic	**2.2287****	**1.7143***	**1.7755***	**1.7137***	**2.3337****
Durbin-Watson test	2.0672	2.0729	2.2626	2.2944	1.8336

***, **, and * indicate statistical significance at the 1%, 5% and 10% levels, respectively.

In models M2 through M5, acquiring companies' return on equity is statistically significant and robust, implying a positive effect of acquirer profitability on shareholders' evaluation of M&A announcements. Given the fact that profitability is a signal for management quality which can be transferred to the target company following the merger, this is not a surprising finding. Contrary, further pressure would be put upon a company that is already in financial distress and that wants to engage in a takeover. Shareholders of profitable companies with good operating performances prior to an M&A transaction can be more assured of merger success in the fashion and leather accessories industry.

In models M3 and M4, we only consider the 131 transactions for which transaction values have been publicly disclosed. In model M3, none of the three additional explanatory variables show statistical significance at any conventional level due to the occurrence of multicollinearity. When we eliminate the relative transaction size criterion in the fourth model, however, the deal size variable becomes significant at the 5% level. This illustrates a positive connection between transaction volumes and bidding shareholder wealth effects.

A possible explanation for this finding could be that large M&A deals are likely to be given top priority status by management and post-merger integration success is taken more seriously than for smaller deals. In addition, substantial operating and cost synergies are more likely to be achieved with larger transactions due to the elimination of redundancies that surface in the manufacturing and distribution divisions of both bidder and target companies. Additionally, the idiosyncratic risk diversification potential is greater for large transactions.

The "100% cash payment" dummy variable and the cash to total assets ratio both have negative signs throughout all models without ever being statistically significant at any level. We therefore cannot support the hypothesis that investors take into account the free cash flows in scenarios where firms with large proportions of cash engage in M&A activities which had been proposed by Jensen (1986) using our cross-sectional regression analysis.

Finally, we apply a fifth model which includes the 71 M&A deals that are denominated as luxury fashion and accessories transactions. We find two remarkable issues. First, the logarithm of the bidder company market capitalization which was highly significant in all previous models, has diminished to almost zero in model M5. Bidder size does not have a significant effect on cumulative abnormal returns in luxury fashion M&A transactions.

Since the "5th bid or higher" dummy is still negative and significant in M5, however, this does not contradict our hypothesis that there is a strongly decreasing marginal utility for companies that undertake many acquisitions. It is rather a consequence of the fact that most publicly listed luxury fashion companies such as LVMH, PPR, Hermès, Christian Dior and Mariella Burani Fashion Group are, on average, large in terms of market capitalization and sales volume. Therefore, size differences do not occur in such magnitudes as in the mid-price segment, resulting in less significant shareholder wealth effects.

The second finding is the strongly negative influence of the P/E ratio of the Datastream World Clothing & Accessories index on transaction CAR. Acquiring shareholders do not welcome luxury fashion M&A deals during phases of high stock market valuations (represented by high index P/E ratios) whereas transactions during times of economic downturn are more positively evaluated by investors. Again, we explain this finding using the free cash flow hypothesis which proposes that transactions during recessionary phases with scarce liquidity are much more cautiously assessed by a company's management than deals that are undertaken during boom years with high levels of disposable free cash flow. Therefore, M&A activity in years with lower P/E ratios is value creating for acquiring shareholders. On the other hand, deals during boom phases are viewed as wasteful investment that is often motivated by managerial overconfidence or hubris behavior as proposed by Croci et al. (2010).

We also control our results for robustness by applying standard ordinary least squares regression instead of the White (1980) test statistic and by using other event windows than the [-1; +1] window as the dependent variable. We further eliminate individual variables from our models to test for the influence of possible multicollinearity between independent variables. Our results, however, do not significantly vary from the findings of our analysis as depicted above.

2.5 CONCLUSION

We analyze wealth effects to bidding shareholders of 192 M&A transactions in the fashion and accessories industry from 1994 to 2009. We find highly significant, positive cumulative abnormal returns for most event windows under consideration. Contrary to most previous cross-industry research, fashion and leather accessories companies benefit from acquiring target firms within their own industry. The observation of different univariate sub-samples shows that a large proportion of value creation is generated by domestic transactions and firms that operate in the mid-price rather than the luxury fashion segment.

Cross-sectional regression analysis further indicates the factors that drive merger success in fashion M&A transactions. As our central finding, the dummy variable "5th bid or higher" and the logarithm of the acquirer's market capitalization have a significantly negative influence on acquirer returns throughout all regression models. We conclude that there is a trade-off between the reduction of fashion companies' inherent idiosyncratic risk exposure via the acquisition of few selective additional brands and the decreasing marginal utility gathered by conducting numerous random acquisitions. This hypothesis is also underlined by the positive and statistically significant influence of the "1st bid" dummy. Furthermore, we find a consistently positive and significant effect of the bidding company's return on equity on transaction CAR which is explained by the additional financial distress and time-consuming efforts that M&A transactions force upon the acquiring company in terms of post-merger integration.

When we isolate luxury fashion deals in our model, we find that the negative acquirer size effect from the previous models diminishes to almost zero which is attributed to generally larger company sizes of publicly listed firms in the luxury industry compared to the mid-price segment. Lastly, we find a strongly negative effect of the price/earnings ratio of the Datastream World Clothing & Accessories index on luxury transaction CAR. We explain this anti-cyclicality with more cautious evaluation of M&A deal considerations by management during periods of economic recession (represented by lower index P/E ratios).

An extended version of this chapter has been published as follows:

Meinshausen, S., & Schiereck, D. (2011). Dressed to Merge – Small Fits Fine: M&A Success in the Fashion and Accessories Industry. *International Review of Financial Analysis, 20* (5), 283-291.

3 OPERATING PERFORMANCE CHANGES FOLLOWING FASHION M&A ACTIVITY

3.1 INTRODUCTION

A substantial part of the empirical research on M&A success focuses on short-term stock price reactions following transaction announcements. While most of these event studies find significantly positive abnormal returns to target shareholders, bidder stockholders gain abnormal returns that range very close around zero. Event studies that also calculate the value implications for combined entities mostly find small positive abnormal returns and therefore conclude that M&A activity, on average, does create value for the parties involved.

A smaller fraction of M&A research analyzes operating performance changes following corporate mergers based on accounting data. In many of such studies, acquiring firms significantly underperform peer group companies in the years after the transaction. This observation represents a clear contradiction to the average results of capital market-oriented event studies. It is therefore of great interest to determine the reasons and drivers of positive stock price reactions and eroding operating performance following corporate mergers.

To compare these two success indicators it is appropriate to control for industry specifics. The fashion and leather accessories industry has seen a tremendous degree of consolidation over the course of the previous decades. There are some unique characteristics that make an independent analysis of this particular business segment worthwhile. First, due to their strong exposure to mostly two seasonal collections' appreciation by their customers and the resulting very short product life cycles, especially small fashion companies face a high business risk. Since risk exposure may well be diversified by acquiring additional brands and thereby stabilizing expected cash flows, M&A activity might appear as a very attractive option to fashion and accessories companies.

Second, unlike many other industries, the balance sheet as well as earnings positions such as EBIT of fashion companies are not as subject to accounting options and valuation scopes. This is mostly due to a very small amount of intangible assets held by fashion and accessories firms. Therefore, we focus our analysis of short- as well as long-term M&A profitability solely on this particular business segment. To the best of our knowledge, a similar analysis has not yet been conducted in both financial and accounting research.

The paper proceeds as follows. Section 3.2 summarizes the results of previous research on stock price reactions and changes in operating performance following mergers and acquisitions. Section 3.3 illustrates the data and methodology applied in our event and accounting studies focusing on transactions in the fashion and accessories industry. Section 3.4 presents and interprets the results of our analyses. Section 3.5 summarizes our findings and concludes.

3.2 LITERATURE OVERVIEW

Empirical research aiming to determine the factors of M&A success has been a large and is a still-growing field throughout the corporate finance literature. A broad overview on the various methodologies and research results is given by Bruner (2002) who identifies four categories of M&A success-related studies. While there are also case studies focusing on single M&A transactions such as Suzuki (2009) on the merger between Turner Broadcasting and Time Warner as well as papers conducting management surveys such as Bassen et al. (2010), the largest part of research on mergers and acquisitions can be divided into two main categories: Capital-market-oriented event studies and accounting studies that analyze merger-related changes in financial statement data.

Since its introduction in a seminal paper by Fama et al. (1969), the event study methodology has become a widely-used instrument to find abnormal stock returns that were induced by corporate events such as earnings announcements, debt and equity issuances as well as mergers and acquisitions. Kothari and Warner (2007) give a comprehensive overview of the large body of applied event studies in the leading finance journals and Corrado (2011) reviews methodological issues and advancements in this field of research.

Concerning the main findings of general cross-industry event studies, there is a growing consensus that corporate mergers significantly enhance target shareholder wealth while bidding stockholders, in most cases, only break even or suffer small, insignificant losses upon the announcement of the transaction. Combined entities normally gain small positive abnormal returns which leads to the conclusion that M&A activity, on average, does enhance shareholder wealth and should therefore be regarded as value-creating. Laabs and Schiereck (2010) also find positive short-term announcement effects in the automotive industry; a long-term buy-and-hold return approach of up to three post-merger years, however, reveals a significant value destruction following M&A. Similar results are also reported by Andrade et al. (2001).

Due to many papers on the theoretical framework, the event study methodology is now widely-standardized, although it still bears a couple of pitfalls. McWilliams and Siegel (1997) identify a lack of capital market efficiency, unanticipated event announcements as well as confounding events as three underlying methodological issues within the assumptions of event study applications. They replicate three event studies and find gravely different results when the issues discussed above are taken into account. Therefore, one should keep in mind that event study results may be biased and should be additionally verified by using other test procedures and methodologies to analyze M&A success.

Accounting studies, on the other hand, are not as well-standardized as event studies, although quite a lot of research activity has also been conducted in this area. Two of the most-cited works are those of Ravenscraft and Scherer (1989) who report a significant drop in operating performance of -2.0% following 471 mergers during the period from 1950 to 1970 as well as Healy et al. (1992) who find a significant increase of 2.8% in accounting performance subsequent to the 50 largest US transactions during 1979 to 1984. These contradictory results are also evident in many other studies. While DeLong (2003) and Ghosh (2001) find negative and Shourun et al. (2011) reports insignificant post-merger operating performance, Hagendorff and Keasey (2009), Cornett et al. (2006) as well as Ramaswamy and Waegelein (2003) observe positive value implications of merger activity on accounting results.

There are also accounting studies that analyze issues related to other financial statement positions. Ghosh and Jain (2000) find a significant rise in acquirers' post-merger financial leverage that is attributed to an increase in firms' debt capacities. La Rocca et al. (2009) additionally argue that diversified firms carry higher debt ratios in order to overcome agency problems such as overinvestment. Dickerson et al. (1997) compare differences between growth rates through external growth via M&A and internal investment opportunities and find a significant underperformance of merging companies to non-acquirers.

Nevertheless, research based on accounting data like event studies is subject to possible inaccuracies. Changes in accounting regulation (Lantto and Sahlström (2009)) and reporting standards (Francis (2010)) for financial statements may bias research results and have to be addressed. Also, the choice of appropriate financial ratios, peer group companies and test statistics must be seriously considered and checked for robustness. Barber and Lyon (1996) analyze many of these issues and give an insightful overview on the explanatory power of test statistics as well as the choice of corresponding benchmark firms for the industry-adjustment of operating performance data.

Some research also aims to determine the interdependence of cumulative abnormal returns (CAR) in event studies and abnormal operating performance (AOP) in accounting studies. Betzer and Goergen (2009) analyze a data sample of 927 US transactions and determine different motives for the four possible types of mergers combining positive and negative CAR as well as positive and negative post-merger accounting performance. Type I mergers (positive CAR and AOP) are motivated by the creation of synergies, type II transactions (positive CAR, negative AOP) are executed to preempt rival companies, type III deals (negative CAR, positive AOP) are undertaken by acquiring companies with overvalued stock prices and type IV mergers (negative CAR and AOP) are attributed to agency problems and hubris behavior.

To the best of our knowledge, there is still no industry-focused comparison of M&A success performance measures. Additionally, there is a lack of conclusive analysis on short-term announcement effects and long-term accounting profitability of fashion mergers. Königs and Schiereck (2008) analyze wealth effects to shareholders of luxury M&A transactions which also includes fashion deals. Their analysis, however, leaves out a substantial amount of M&A conducted in the lower price segment and, even more important, a more long-term oriented and accounting-based perspective on merger profitability.

In this paper, we first calculate the short-term wealth effects accruing to bidding shareholders of fashion and accessories M&A transactions. In a next step, we analyze the changes in operating performance and financial leverage following these transactions as well as the sales growth rates of external growth via mergers and acquisitions versus internal growth opportunities via project investments. We use a set of financial ratios and an industry-adjusted methodology to detect abnormal operating performance derived from the existing accounting study literature. In doing so, we hope to gain an in-depth knowledge of M&A profitability in the fashion industry from both a short-term, capital market-oriented as well as a long-term, accounting-based perspective.

3.3 DATA AND METHODOLOGY

3.3.1 Data

We use the SDC/Thomson One Banker Deals database in order to identify all relevant fashion and leather accessories M&A transactions that have been conducted between 1 January 1994 and 31 December 2007. The following criteria are applied to the search engine to filter relevant M&A deals:

(1) Both the acquirer and target company have a primary SIC code within the major groups "23 – Apparel And Other Finished Products Made From Fabrics And Similar Materials" or "56 – Apparel And Accessory Stores".

(2) The bidder company is a publicly listed entity and liquid daily trading data for 273 trading days preceding and 20 trading days following the event date is available.

(3) Financial statement data for three fiscal years prior to and following the transaction is available on the SDC/Thomson One Banker Company Analysis database.

(4) The status of the transaction is "completed".

(5) A controlling stake (>50% of voting shares) has been acquired in the transaction.

Criterion (1) determines that private equity transactions and financial investments are excluded from our sample. In order to conduct our event and accounting study, sufficient stock price and financial statement data has to be available, hence criteria (2) and (3). Criteria (4) and (5) further remove withdrawn or pending transactions as well as minority block purchases from our analysis. The final sample consists of 160 M&A transactions that meet all of these criteria. Table 3.1 illustrates some of the sample companies' key financials.

Table 3.1: Key financials and ratios of acquiring companies

COMPANY FINANCIALS	MEAN	MEDIAN	MIN	MAX	SKEWNESS	STANDARD DEVIATION
Market capitalization (in $m)	5,065.96	1,943.07	26.17	52,250.08	2.96	8,447.18
Sales (in $m)	3,200.30	1,521.29	10.37	24,102.59	2.51	4,170.53
EBITDA (in $m)	531.35	223.11	-25.46	4,067.36	2.29	719.82
EBIT (in $m)	427.60	183.49	-55.75	3,259.45	2.29	575.22
Total assets (in $m)	3,681.13	1,177.56	30.92	35,081.44	3.06	6,158.99
Cash to total assets (in %)	13.69%	10.27%	0.31%	58.62%	1.48	12.12%
Debt to total assets (in %)	22.11%	20.67%	0.00%	58.70%	0.50	13.25%
Market-to-book ratio (x)	2.67x	2.35x	0.50x	10.28x	1.97	1.54x
Free cash flow (in $m)	338.53	131.96	-42.84	2,521.08	2.29	459.14

Balance sheet items in table 3.1 are taken from the end of the fiscal year preceding the transaction announcement. The data show a concentration of medium-sized businesses with a strong potential for free cash flow generation. Skewness measures and differences between means and medians indicate that some financials such as the size criteria of market capitalization, sales and total assets are not evenly distributed and moderately skewed right.

We further need to determine all relevant peer group companies for our sample firms to estimate industry-adjusted abnormal operating performance. We use the following criteria to identify these peer group companies:

(1) The company also has a primary SIC code starting with "23" or "56".

(2) The company has not conducted relevant M&A deals within the fashion and accessories industry during the period from 1994 to 2007.

(3) Financial statement data is available for fiscal years 1991 to 2009.

(4) Sales volume and total assets exceeded $500m in fiscal year 2009.

Criterion (1) determines that peer group companies operate in the same industry as sample firms. We also conduct internet research to verify the correctness of industry classifications and to avoid misspecifications. Calculating abnormal operating performance induced by M&A, criterion (2) demands that peer firms did not participate in the takeover market during the event and accounting study time window. Otherwise, the respective company would have been taken into the acquiring firm data sample.

As for sample companies, accounting data for three years prior to and following transactions also have to be available for peer group firms, hence criterion (3). Lastly, since means and medians of sample companies' pre-merger financials are comparably high (see table 3.1), criterion (4) assigns a minimum peer group company size as measured in terms of both sales and book value of total assets of at least $500m each at the end of fiscal year 2009.

We also determine relevant financial ratios for the measurement of operating performance, financial leverage and corporate growth. Since there is no distinct consensus about the best-suited figures, we apply three ratios of operating profitability and financial leverage each. Our first ratio of operating performance is operating cash flow (OCF) to book value of assets (Healy et al. (1992)). OCF is defined as sales (SDC/Thomson One Banker database item no. 01001) minus cost of goods sold (item 01051), and selling, general and administrative expenses (item 01101) plus depreciation, amortization and depletion (item 01151). OCF is then scaled by the book value of total assets (item 02999).

Betzer and Goergen (2009), however, argue that both book and market values of assets may be systematically biased due to accounting options and market value decreases following M&A transactions, respectively. In line with Ramaswamy and Waegelein (2003), we therefore also scale operating cash flows as defined above by the market value of assets (item 18100) as a check for robustness. As a third ratio, we also use return on equity (item 08301) as an additional measure of operating performance in our analysis.

Total debt (item 03255) to firm value (as defined as book value of debt plus market value of equity (item 08001)) is used as our first measure of financial leverage. We further calculate the ratio of interest expense on debt (item 01251) to operating cash flow as an additional measure (Ghosh and Jain (2000)). Additionally, we also compute the traditional debt ratio of total debt to total assets. As an appropriate measure for corporate growth, we find that sales growth may be the best-suited figure due to its considerably smaller exposure to accounting options compared to growth rates of earnings or total assets measures.

3.3.2 Methodology

In order to analyze short-term announcement effects of fashion and accessories M&A transactions, we use standard event study methodology. We retrieve daily stock and corresponding equity indices returns that have been adjusted for dividend payments and changes to the capital structure from Thomson Financial Datastream. We use an event window length of 41 trading days, starting 20 days prior to and ending 20 days after the transaction announcement. The estimation period consists of 252 trading days (one full trading year) before the event window and is used to calculate the ordinary least squares regression coefficients for the measurement of expected stock price performance.

We choose the market model as an estimator of cumulative abnormal returns as defined as the difference between actual and expected returns for each company *j* (Brown and Warner (1980)). We then use the parametric standard t-test statistic, the heteroscedasticity-consistent test statistic of Boehmer et al. (1991) as well as a non-parametric Wilcoxon signed-rank test for medians to test our results for statistical significance at conventional levels.

As a first step of our accounting study, we compare the raw values of pre- and post-merger ratios of operating performance, financial leverage and sales growth for the three fiscal years preceding and three fiscal years following the transaction. We then calculate the differences between the averages for the three and two years prior to and after the transaction, respectively, as well as the difference between the last year before and the first year after the transaction. These differences are tested for statistical significance using a standard t-test statistic for means as well as a Wilcoxon signed-rank test for medians.

In a next step, we use our non-acquirer industry peer group to detect abnormal operating performance following the approach of Barber and Lyon (1996) who find that test statistics are best-specified when based on matched firms with similar pre-event performance. We therefore match each sample company with the entire size-matched peer group as well as the same peer group quintile of performance one year prior to the respective transaction. Expected performance is calculated as the intercept α of a cross-sectional regression of post-merger ratios for each company *j* after subtracting the industry median ($ratio^{ind\text{-}adj}_{post,j}$) on the respective industry-adjusted pre-merger ratios ($ratio^{ind\text{-}adj}_{pre,j}$):

$$(1)\ Ratio^{ind\text{-}adj}_{post,\,j} = \alpha + \beta * ratio^{ind\text{-}adj}_{pre,j} + \varepsilon_j$$

Abnormal operating performance for each company *j* is measured as the difference between actual and expected performance for each year. Medians for size- and performance-matched abnormal operating performance are tested for statistical significance using the Wilcoxon signed-rank test. As a robustness check, we also test means of abnormal performance using a simple t-test statistic.

Finally, we apply cross-sectional regression analysis to determine the key drivers of accounting performance following M&A transactions in the fashion industry. We use the performance-matched abnormal operating performance as defined as OCF to book value of assets for each transaction in year [+1] as the dependent variable. We then use a set of various criteria as independent variables to estimate their influence on the sample companies' operating performance. The independent variables "luxury transaction", "cross-border transaction" and "100% cash payment" are binary dummy variables that take on the value 1 if they apply to the respective deal and the value 0 if not. The variables "1st bid" and "5th bid or higher" are also binary variables that take on the value 1 if the transaction is either the first or the fifth or higher M&A deal executed by a company in our observation period (Fuller et al. (2002)).

We use a series of acquirer- and transaction-specific criteria including deal size, logarithm of market capitalization, cash to total assets and market-to-book ratio as independent variables. To analyze the influence of financial leverage on merger success, we also apply both the pre- and post-merger debt ratio from one fiscal year prior to [-1] and one fiscal year following the transaction [+1]. Abnormal sales growth is defined as the size-matched abnormal sales growth for the third post-merger year [+3]. Relative transaction size is defined as deal value divided by acquirer market capitalization on the announcement day.

The rebased price/earnings (P/E) ratio of the Datastream World Clothing & Accessories index is used as an estimator of the stock market valuation level and hence the economic climate in which a transaction is executed. We also use this equity index and the corresponding Datastream World Market index to calculate cumulative abnormal returns to the fashion and leather accessories industry as a reaction to the announcements of our sample transactions. This is in line with Betzer and Goergen (2009) who use a similar parameter as their primary indicator of the preemption motive for corporate mergers that result in stock price increases and consecutive drops in operating performance.

We apply five different models in our cross-sectional regression. Models M1 and M2 include the entire sample of 160 transactions, models M3 and M4 take into account all 111 transactions for which deal values have been disclosed. Model M5 consists of 59 transactions that are labeled as luxury deals. We test all five models using the heteroscedasticity-consistent test statistic of White (1980) with adjusted standard errors and a standard OLS regression model as a check for robustness of our results.

3.4 RESULTS

3.4.1 Short-term announcement effects

Table 3.2 shows the main results of our short-term event study. Similar to the results reported in chapter 2, there are significantly positive value implications for M&A announcements in the fashion industry. Our results are robust across different event windows and test statistics. This implies an optimistic evaluation of corporate mergers by the shareholders of fashion and accessories companies. In the following, we therefore analyze whether these optimistic expectations are also consecutively met by the post-merger accounting performance.

Table 3.2: Event study results for fashion M&A data sample transactions

EVENT WINDOW	CUMULATIVE ABNORMAL RETURN		T-TEST	BOEHMER-TEST	WILCOXON SIGNED-RANK TEST
Days (t)	Mean	Median	t-value	z-score	z-score
[-20;+20]	1.03%	0.33%	0.921	0.770	-0.340
[-10;+10]	1.43%	0.74%	1.736*	1.739*	-1.470
[-5;+5]	1.16%	0.41%	1.873*	1.835*	-1.199
[-1;+1]	1.06%	0.71%	3.111***	3.152***	-3.000***
[0;+0]	0.81%	0.21%	2.953***	3.053***	-2.104**
[0;+1]	1.03%	0.69%	3.201***	3.300***	-3.458***
[0;+5]	1.25%	0.51%	2.424**	2.528**	-1.819*
[0;+10]	1.01%	0.22%	1.897*	2.013**	-1.400
[0;+20]	0.82%	0.93%	1.050	1.110	-0.804

***, **, and * indicate statistical significance at the 1%, 5%, and 10% levels, respectively.

3.4.2. *Cash flow returns and profitability*

First, we observe our three profitability measures over the period of three years preceding and following the merger. Year dates are measured relative to the transaction, year [-1] e.g. represents the last year prior to the deal execution. Means and medians of the raw values for all sample companies are reported and tested for statistical significance in table 3.3.

Table 3.3: Raw measures of pre- and post-merger operating performance

RAW MEASURES OF OPERATING PERFORMANCE						
	OCF / BV OF ASSETS		OCF / MV OF ASSETS		RETURN ON EQUITY	
Year	Mean	Median	Mean	Median	Mean	Median
-3	23.05%	19.93%	17.38%	13.54%	12.83%	14.71%
-2	21.74%	19.24%	15.34%	13.60%	15.44%	16.03%
-1	20.22%	18.73%	14.72%	12.95%	15.72%	15.75%
+1	18.99%	16.63%	12.63%	12.37%	14.35%	15.05%
+2	19.26%	16.95%	14.22%	13.56%	11.39%	13.90%
+3	18.35%	17.44%	14.71%	13.61%	8.34%	11.76%
Difference between averages of years [-3; -1] and years [+1; +3]						
	-2.80% ***	-2.30% ***	-1.96% *	-0.18%	-3.30% **	-1.93% **
Difference between averages of years [-2; -1] and years [+1; +2]						
	-1.85% **	-2.20% **	-1.60%	-0.31%	-2.71% **	-1.42% **
Difference between means/medians for years [-1] and [+1]						
	-1.23%	-2.10%	-2.09% *	-0.57% **	-1.37%	-0.71%

***, **, and * indicate statistical significance at the 1%, 5%, and 10% levels, respectively.

We see a considerable drop in raw operating performance of up to -3.30% throughout all ratios and observation windows. Test results are statistically significant especially for the OCF to book value of assets and return on equity measures. OCF to market value of assets also shows comparably high negative means, although it is not as statistically significant. This might well caused by a higher volatility and thereby higher standard deviation in market values of assets compared to the more stable book values (see table 3.1). In a next step, we apply our industry benchmark to adjust the results for abnormal operating performance. Table 3.4 reports medians for the three ratios with size- and performance-matched results. We rely on medians solemnly since Barber and Lyon (1996) show that the Wilcoxon signed-rank test is generally better-suited to detect abnormal performance than parametric test statistics.

Table 3.4: Industry-adjusted abnormal operating performance

	INDUSTRY-ADJUSTED MEASURES OF OPERATING PERFORMANCE					
	OCF / BV OF ASSETS		OCF / MV OF ASSETS		RETURN ON EQUITY	
Year	Size-matched	Perf-matched	Size-matched	Perf-matched	Size-matched	Perf-matched
-3	0.35%	0.16%	0.75% **	0.88% ***	-0.61%	0.05%
-2	0.83% ***	-0.13%	0.39%	0.41% *	0.58%	0.28%
-1	-0.02%	-0.55% ***	0.03%	0.08%	0.70% **	0.11%
+1	-1.27% ***	-1.15% ***	-1.22% ***	-1.09% ***	0.79%	0.66%
+2	-0.78% **	-0.61% **	-0.69%	0.09%	-1.18%	-0.74%
+3	-1.13% ***	-0.67% **	1.81% **	1.17% *	-2.70% ***	-2.99% ***
Difference between averages of years [-3; -1] and years [+1; +3]						
	-1.45% ***	-0.63% **	-0.42%	-0.40%	-1.25% ***	-1.17% ***
Difference between averages of years [-2; -1] and years [+1; +2]						
	-1.43% ***	-0.54% *	-1.17% *	-0.75% **	-0.83% **	-0.24% *
Difference between medians for years [-1] and [+1]						
	-1.25% ***	-0.60% *	-1.25% *	-1.18% **	0.10%	0.55% *

***, **, and * indicate statistical significance at the 1%, 5%, and 10% levels, respectively.

Industry-adjusted results also show a statistically significant decrease in operating performance with a slightly smaller magnitude of up to -1.45%. OCF measures especially show a strong post-merger underperformance of bidder firms as compared to their non-acquirer peer group companies. It is of further interest that performance does not recover in a timely manner following the transactions which is most obvious for the return on equity measure that is strongly negative and significant at the 1% level for the third post-merger year for both size and performance-matched statistics. We finally checked our results for robustness using means of abnormal operating performance instead of medians. The results do not vary from our findings while mean values are generally even higher in magnitude than median results.

These findings mark a clear contradiction to the results of our event study which finds significantly positive cumulative abnormal returns to shareholders of bidding fashion companies. The fact that mergers often cause share price increases and subsequent drops in operating performance has been explained by Fridolfsson and Stennek (2005) who introduce the concept of the preemption merger motive. According to their theory, mergers in an industry of high consolidation likely induce negative industry effects to rival firms that have not been able to bid for the target company. From a capital market-oriented point of view, it is therefore better to be an insider, i.e. to be part of the merger, rather than not to participate in the transaction at all. Increasing share prices, however, do not necessarily affect operating performance which may explain the dissonance between stock price and accounting performance reactions. In our cross-sectional regression analysis, we will also analyze whether the preemption motive may have been a driver of merger decisions in the fashion industry.

3.4.3 Changes in financial leverage

To analyze the changes in financial leverage associated with fashion mergers, we also first observe our three pre- and post-merger raw financial leverage ratios for all sample companies. Due to extreme outliers, we winsorize the results of the interest expense to operating cash flow ratio at the 1st and 99th percentiles. The results of our analysis are shown in table 3.5.

Table 3.5: Raw measures of pre- and post-merger financial leverage

RAW MEASURES OF FINANCIAL LEVERAGE						
	DEBT/FIRM VALUE		DEBT RATIO		INTEREST EXP./OCF	
Year	Mean	Median	Mean	Median	Mean	Median
-3	19.84%	14.94%	23.72%	21.63%	12.26%	7.57%
-2	18.88%	13.64%	23.39%	20.45%	9.81%	6.71%
-1	18.04%	13.14%	22.11%	20.67%	9.02%	6.60%
+1	20.47%	14.52%	25.14%	21.69%	10.77%	8.30%
+2	22.73%	18.63%	25.88%	24.11%	15.05%	8.82%
+3	24.81%	20.08%	25.77%	24.58%	15.62%	8.48%
Difference between averages of years [-3; -1] and years [+1; +3]						
	3.75% ***	3.84% ***	2.52% **	2.54% *	3.45% *	1.57%
Difference between averages of years [-2; -1] and years [+1; +2]						
	3.14% ***	3.19% **	2.76% ***	2.34% **	3.50% **	1.90% **
Difference between means/medians for years [-1] and [+1]						
	2.43% ***	1.38% **	3.03% ***	1.02% ***	1.75% ***	1.69%

***, **, and * indicate statistical significance at the 1%, 5%, and 10% levels, respectively.

We find a highly significant increase in all financial leverage measures from the first post-merger year on to the third year following the transaction. Increases in debt to firm value are up to 3.75% and significant at the 1% level. The results for the interest expense to operating cash flow ratio are not entirely as significant as the other measures due to higher standard deviations, although they still support our finding of a sharp post-merger increase in leverage for fashion companies. In the following, we also adjust our results for industry-wide leverage effects and report abnormal financial leverage in table 3.6.

Table 3.6: Industry-adjusted abnormal financial leverage

INDUSTRY-ADJUSTED MEASURES OF FINANCIAL LEVERAGE						
	DEBT/FIRM VALUE		DEBT RATIO		INTEREST EXP./OCF	
Year	Size-matched	Perf-matched	Size-matched	Perf-matched	Size-matched	Perf-matched
-3	0.49% **	2.11% ***	0.75% *	0.59%	0.16%	0.10%
-2	0.00%	0.34%	0.06%	0.03%	-0.11%	-0.18% *
-1	0.31%	-1.09%	-0.10%	-0.14%	-0.40% **	-0.57% ***
+1	-0.33%	-0.34%	0.00%	0.00%	-0.43%	-0.46%
+2	0.03% ***	0.00% ***	0.44% *	1.13% **	0.02%	-0.13%
+3	2.37% ***	3.19% ***	0.23% *	0.00% **	0.34% **	0.21% **
Difference between averages of years [-3; -1] and years [+1; +3]						
	0.42% ***	0.50%	-0.02%	0.21%	0.09% ***	0.09% ***
Difference between averages of years [-2; -1] and years [+1; +2]						
	-0.30% *	0.21%	0.24% *	0.62%	0.05% **	0.08% ***
Difference between medians for years [-1] and [+1]						
	-0.63%	0.76%	0.10% ***	0.14% *	-0.03%	0.10% *

***, **, and * indicate statistical significance at the 1%, 5%, and 10% levels, respectively.

Medians for industry-adjusted abnormal financial leverage measures are generally not as high in magnitude as in our pre- and post-merger sample company comparison. Still, the results underline our key findings of increased financial leverage after M&A transactions in the fashion industry. The results also comply with the study of Ghosh and Jain (2000) who find a similar rise in financial leverage and explain these results with a post-merger increase in acquiring firms' debt capacities. They argue that debt capacity is likely to be higher following corporate mergers due to a corresponding increase in firm size, a reduction in the combined entity's earnings variability and therefore lower default risk.

Ghosh and Jain (2000) also assume that merging companies might have unused debt capacities in the years preceding the merger, yet they cannot verify this hypothesis based on their statistical results. In the following, we do not discuss the reasons for the increase in post-merger financial leverage, but rather focus on the implications of higher debt ratios for the operating performance of acquiring firms following fashion transactions. We apply both pre- and post-merger debt ratios as independent variables in our cross-sectional regression analysis to analyze their influence on operating performance.

3.4.4 Sales growth of M&A and internal investments

We further compare growth opportunities by external growth by M&A to internal growth by investments in corporate projects. While M&A seems to be an opportunity to enhance firm size quickly, we also evaluate the sustainability of accelerated growth by M&A as opposed to more long-term, project-oriented internal investment opportunities. We follow the same approach as for operating performance and financial leverage and first analyze both pre- and post-merger sales growth rates for sample companies on a stand-alone basis and apply industry-adjusted abnormal sales growth with the help of our size- and performance-matched peer group afterwards. We winsorize our results at the 1st and 99th percentiles to account for extreme outliers. Table 3.7 reports our results.

Table 3.7: Raw and industry-adjusted abnormal sales growth rates

	SALES GROWTH					
	RAW SALES GROWTH		ABNORMAL SALES GROWTH			
			SIZE-MATCHED		PERF-MATCHED	
Year	Mean	Median	Mean	Median	Mean	Median
-3	8.71%	8.40%	2.56%	-0.16%	4.31%	-0.67%
-2	9.01%	8.80%	-0.49%	-0.44%	5.22% *	0.84%
-1	14.50%	9.38%	5.66% **	1.86% *	5.80%	2.26% **
ø	10.74%	8.86%	2.58%	0.42%	5.11% *	0.81%
+1	18.77%	11.41%	7.82% **	4.52% ***	9.18% ***	3.62% ***
+2	15.59%	9.69%	7.23% ***	1.00% *	7.23% ***	1.02%
+3	8.09%	4.64%	-4.82% **	-6.35% ***	-5.40% **	-5.00% ***
ø	14.15%	8.58%	3.41% *	-0.28%	3.67% **	-0.12%
Difference between averages of years [-3; -1] and years [+1; +3]						
	3.41% *	-0.28%	0.83%	-0.69%	-1.44%	-0.93%
Difference between averages of years [-2; -1] and years [+1; +2]						
	5.43% **	1.46% **	4.94% **	2.05% *	2.70%	0.77% *
Difference between means for years [-1] and [+1]						
	4.27%	2.03%	2.16%	2.67%	3.38%	1.36%

***, **, and * indicate statistical significance at the 1%, 5%, and 10% levels, respectively.

Not surprisingly, we find a statistically significant jump in sales growth rates in the first year following the merger for both means and medians of our industry-adjusted analysis. While means for abnormal growth rates in the second post-merger year are still very high, the corresponding medians do not show statistical significance. On the contrary, abnormal sales growth for the third year after the merger shows a highly negative and statistically significant trend that is robust across means and medians as well as size- and performance-matched benchmark portfolios. Abnormal sales growth rates are up to -6.35% in year [+3], giving a clear indication that positive abnormal growth rates of the first two years following the merger cannot be sustained by acquiring companies.

These results comply with those of Dickerson et al. (1997) who also find that corporate growth via internal investment opportunities yields higher rates of return than growth achieved through M&A activity. When we compare the averages of abnormal sales growth rates of the three years preceding and following the transaction, we see a negative difference in three out of four observations of up to -1.44%. In addition to our negative post-merger operating performance results, these findings further emphasize our negative outlook on merger profitability in the fashion and leather accessories industry.

3.4.5 *Cross-sectional regression analysis*

Having analyzed the value implications of fashion and accessories M&A transactions on accounting performance measures, we further seek to determine the drivers of acquiring companies' post-merger operating performance. We use the performance-matched abnormal operating cash flow to book value of assets ratio for the first post-merger year [+1] as the dependent variable. We apply five models using different criteria as explanatory variables in our cross-sectional regression analysis. Results are reported in table 3.8.

The cash to total assets ratio shows a significantly negative influence of pre-merger cash availability on post-merger operating performance. This can be seen as a confirmation of the free cash flow hypothesis. Excess cash disposability may lead to a less cautious evaluation of merger decisions by managers and therefore also affect the resulting operating performance due to a weak emphasis on post-merger integration. On the contrary, firms with sparse cash resources need to weigh potential risks and benefits of mergers and acquisitions a lot more seriously since M&A deals put additional stress upon the acquiring firm and demand strong management attention as well as financial and time resources that could otherwise be concentrated on operational issues.

Table 3.8: Results of cross-sectional regression analysis

MODEL	M1	M2	M3	M4	M5
INTERCEPT	**0.1428***	0.0932	0.1771	0.1258	**0.2290*****
	(1.9306)	(1.1242)	(1.6584)	(1.0885)	(2.7188)
DUMMY VARIABLES					
Luxury transaction	0.0144	-0.0052	0.0277	0.0202	
	(0.7593)	-(0.2569)	(1.3002)	(0.8816)	
Cross-border transaction	0.0123	0.0167	0.0314	**0.0418***	0.0280
	(0.8134)	(1.0152)	(1.6089)	(1.8647)	(1.0612)
1st bid	-0.0271	-0.0298	**-0.0669***	**-0.0776****	0.0185
	-(1.0631)	-(1.1124)	-(1.9157)	-(2.0490)	(0.5693)
5th bid or higher	-0.0223	-0.0266	**-0.0606****	**-0.0679****	0.0047
	-(1.0710)	-(1.1620)	-(2.3863)	-(2.3144)	(0.2321)
DEAL CHARACTERISTICS					
Deal value			0.0000	0.0000	
			-(0.4279)	-(0.6577)	
Relative transaction size			0.0252	0.0210	
			(0.6048)	(0.4911)	
100% cash payment			-0.0227	-0.0235	
			-(1.1477)	-(1.1560)	
ACQUIRER FINANCIALS					
Log market cap	-0.0057	0.0048	0.0248	0.0336	-0.0142
	-(0.3054)	(0.2601)	(0.8893)	(1.1739)	-(2.6414)
Abnormal sales growth	-0.0839	-0.0695	-0.1120	-0.0951	-0.1007
	-(1.1037)	-(0.8733)	-(1.4217)	-(1.1454)	-(1.3862)
Cash to total assets	**-0.3012*****	**-0.2472****	**-0.3024****	**-0.2358****	**-0.3597*****
	-(2.7471)	-(2.4103)	-(2.2029)	-(2.0062)	-(2.9416)
Market-to-book ratio	0.0089	0.0063	-0.0036	-0.0076	0.0006
	(1.1477)	(0.7316)	-(0.4009)	-(0.7668)	(0.0636)
Pre-merger debt ratio		-0.1292		-0.1807	
		-(1.1836)		-(1.3617)	
Post-merger debt ratio	**-0.2085****		**-0.2192****		-0.0602
	-(2.3869)		-(2.3428)		-(0.4749)
CYCLICALITY					
DS World Clothing P/E ratio	**-0.0036***	**-0.0035***	**-0.0067****	**-0.0061****	**-0.0070****
	-(1.6592)	-(1.6599)	-(2.6181)	-(2.3756)	-(2.6414)
Industry CAR	-0.8000	-0.8494	-1.7943	-1.6803	-0.9384
	-(0.9611)	-(1.0084)	-(1.6476)	-(1.5451)	-(1.1248)
N	160	160	111	111	59
Adj. R^2	0.1101	0.0662	0.1831	0.1413	0.1957
F-statistic	**2.6409*****	**1.9585****	**2.6441*****	**2.2246****	**2.2642****
Durbin-Watson test	1.6236	1.5758	2.0104	2.0265	2.3868

***, ** and * indicate statistical significance at the 1%, 5% and 10% levels, respectively.

An additional finding of our analysis that underlines the need for critical examination of merger decisions is the strongly negative effect of stock market valuation levels on operating performance. High price/earnings ratios of the Datastream World Clothing & Accessories index indicate periods of economic upswing which lead to deteriorating accounting performance following M&A deals. This again shows that deals which were executed in downturn markets and scarce resources (represented by low P/E ratios) significantly outperform mergers that were undertaken during boom phases. According to our analysis, selective and well-considered M&A deals generally have a more optimistic outlook of positive operating performance development than random, all cash-financed bull-market takeovers that were mostly executed for the purpose of increasing firm size and thereby management status and reputation.

First bid transactions do not show clearly different operating performance than fifth or higher bids. This may be caused by the fact that first-time acquirers are not well-acquainted with post-merger integration and therefore are often not able to realize anticipated synergies. We further cannot verify the suggested preemption motive for the transactions since industry CAR are not significant at any conventional level in our models. Although some mergers such as e.g. PPR's acquisition of Gucci that was preceded by a takeover battle with rival conglomerate LVMH may have well been motivated by preemption considerations, this generally cannot be substantiated for all sample transactions.

We further investigate the influence of pre- and post-merger debt ratios on fashion acquirers' abnormal operating performance. While pre-merger debt ratios as reported in the last fiscal year prior to the transaction do not show a significant influence on abnormal cash flow returns, post-merger debt ratios from the first year following the transaction have statistically significant negative implications for the accounting performance. We apply pre- and post-merger debt ratios in separate models due to high potential multicollinearity.

This is a rather puzzling finding since financial leverage increases following corporate mergers are widely anticipated throughout the literature and, in most cases, emphasis is placed on its positive consequences such as agency benefits of corporate debt and tax deductibility of interest payments. According to our analysis, however, there seem to be negative implications of corporate indebtedness that outweigh these beneficial outcomes of increased leverage.

In general, it is assumed that there is an optimal level of corporate debt that perfectly balances agency benefits and agency costs of debt. The former consist of advantages resulting from the tax shield as well as managerial incentives while the latter persist in bankruptcy and financial distress costs. Since there is a statistically significant negative effect of post-merger debt ratios on operating performance of acquiring firms, it could be concluded that some of the sample companies increased their leverage beyond that optimal point so that agency costs outweigh agency benefits of debt.

Contrarily, firms with lower debt ratios achieve significantly better operating performance following mergers. We therefore conclude that fashion mergers do indeed result in an increase in debt capacity for bidding companies; it should nevertheless be carefully assessed whether a full utilization of these capacities is eventually beneficial for post-merger operating performance. Increased financial leverage puts additional stress on firms that are already financially and temporally preoccupied with post-merger integration.

3.5 CONCLUSION

We compare cumulative abnormal stock returns and abnormal operating performance following 160 bidder M&A deals in the fashion and accessories industry from 1994 to 2007. While acquiring shareholders earn significantly positive abnormal returns upon announcement of the transactions, there is a significant drop in operating performance in the three fiscal years following the merger. We report robust results for our findings throughout various size- and performance-matched models of abnormal operating performance using three different performance measures. These contradictory results of stock price and operating performance reactions represent a puzzling finding for fashion mergers and give a mixed outlook on merger profitability in this particular industry.

We further investigate the development of leverage ratios following fashion mergers and find a significant increase in three different post-merger leverage ratios. This is attributed to a general increase in debt capacity which is due to larger firm size and reduced earnings volatility as direct consequences of M&A transactions. Nevertheless, cross-sectional regression analysis reveals that increased debt ratios have a significantly negative influence on post-merger operating performance. We conclude that this might be caused by financial leverage increases beyond the optimal point of corporate indebtedness. While debt financing can be seen as a signal for management quality and offers advantages from the tax shield, higher interest payments on debt put additional stress on companies that are already engaged in costly and time-consuming post-merger integration activities. The utilization level of increased debt capacities should therefore be carefully assessed by acquiring companies.

As an additional indicator of merger advantageousness, we analyze sales growth for pre- and post-merger years. While it comes to no surprise that sales growth is considerably higher for acquiring companies in the first post-merger fiscal year than for benchmark firms, these accelerated growth rates cannot be sustained over the course of the observation period. In the third post-merger year, growth rates of bidding companies significantly underperform non-acquirer peers. Therefore, it cannot be concluded that external growth via merger activities is generally favorable to growth achieved by internal project investments. This finding contributes to our rather pessimistic outlook on the profitability of M&A in the fashion and leather accessories industry.

4 DIVESTITURES, THE INSOLVENCY OF ESCADA AND BEHAVIORAL FINANCE

4.1 INTRODUCTION

During the first two decades since its foundation in 1976, Munich-based haute couture and prêt-à-porter luxury fashion brand ESCADA AG participated repeatedly in the takeover market to support its growth strategy, creating a diversified portfolio of ladies' fashion and accessories brands and product lines. While revenues grew steadily, the company's profitability became weak. Due to a series of operating and strategic deficits as well as macroeconomic crises at the beginning of the 21st century, management agreed upon a corporate refocusing on ESCADA's core competencies in the luxury fashion market.

While most of the company's non-core segments were in fact subsequently divested, management for some reason adhered to PRIMERA AG, the company's single most important mid-price ladies' fashion business line. Upon the decision for the refocusing strategy in fiscal year 2000/2001, PRIMERA AG which included the four brands apriori, BiBA, cavita and Laurèl accounted for roughly one quarter of ESCADA's total sales volume. In spite of management's continuous assurance of its divestiture plans for PRIMERA, ESCADA invested heavily in the non-core segment over the course of the following years and kept hold of it for almost an entire decade. The final divestiture process was not initiated until ESCADA finally faced serious financial distress at the end of 2008.

Since management realized the positive implications of a potential disposal at an early stage and independent broker reports consented on a lucrative standalone value range of between €150m and €200m for the PRIMERA segment, it is difficult to view management's behavior as an unbiased rational decision-making process. To describe and understand management non-actions we refer to some insights of behavioral finance. We show how key findings of behavioral finance such as loss aversion, status quo bias and escalating commitment can help to explain ESCADA's heavily belated disposal policy.

These psychological components in the decision-making process significantly altered management's assessment of the PRIMERA business and led to a prolonged disposal hesitation that seriously affected ESCADA's liquidity. In addition to the absence of an efficient market for corporate control, this can be seen as one of the most important reasons for the company's bankruptcy in 2009.

The paper proceeds as follows. Section 4.2 gives an overview of behavioral finance literature. It focuses mainly on the implications of loss aversion and status quo bias for corporate decision-making processes. Section 4.3 briefly illustrates the history of ESCADA AG and then describes the PRIMERA divestment case during the years 2000 to 2009 in a distinctive three-phase pattern. We use evidence from ESCADA annual reports and ad-hoc announcements to illustrate the relevance of decision-making biases that can be observed in this divestiture process. Section 4.4 summarizes our findings and concludes.

4.2 LITERATURE OVERVIEW

One of the central assumptions of neoclassical economic theory is rational behavior of all participants in the market. Accordingly, individuals make choices based on rational preferences to maximize individual utility while companies use rational choices to maximize cash flows. A series of major economic events such as stock market crashes, corporate bankruptcies and excessive acquisition premiums paid in the takeover market led to the conclusion, however, that this assumption does not always describe managers' behavior in financial decision-making processes and that market participants also follow subjective and sometimes irrational rules (Shiller (2000)). Since the beginning of the second half of the 20th century the influence of psychological effects on investment and financing decisions has therefore been extensively analyzed.

Early criticism of the rational behavior hypothesis was offered by Allais (1953). Allais argued that the expected utility hypothesis does not represent a realistic model to describe human behavior in decision-making processes under uncertainty and that "objective" probabilities could be significantly altered by subjective expectations of market participants. In what was later named the "Allais paradox", he described a decision problem that foreshadowed one of the central insights of behavioral finance, the S-shaped value function and the thereby implied different perception of gains and losses by individuals. Among others such as Becker (1962), Allais marked an important critique of the prevalence of the rational individual behavior assumption and thereby paved the way for the further development of behavioral finance theory.

Kahneman and Tversky (1979) introduced prospect theory, an alternative model to expected utility theory that was based on Allais' ideas. They assumed that people perceive possible outcomes of a decision problem as gains and losses relative to a specified reference point rather than final states of wealth. The value function of prospect theory is determined by two effects. First, the certainty effect describes the tendency to prefer certain positive outcomes with lower utility levels to uncertain (or risky) positive outcomes with higher expected utilities. This effect is also known as risk aversion and determines the concave part of the value function above the reference point (above zero or "gains").

Second, the reflection effect mirrors this certainty effect below the reference point (below zero or "losses") and therefore determines a convex course of the value function. This functional form implies that people prefer higher uncertain (or risky) losses to lower certain losses. This effect can therefore also be described as risk seeking. Due to these two effects, the value function of prospect theory follows an S-shaped course. The implications of this model have been further discussed e.g. by Barberis et al. (2006) and Barberis et al. (2001).

The concept of loss aversion was subsequently discussed in greater detail by Thaler (1980), who describes loss aversion as a basic human inadequacy to deal with experienced losses and the difficulty of admitting personal failures. As an important factor in decision problems, Thaler points out the influence of sunk costs. Although sunk costs should be irrelevant in the evaluation of an investment opportunity (since they cannot be retrieved), people tend to value goods or services higher if there are sunk costs involved (e.g. a fitness club membership). The sunk costs effect can also be applied to decision situations concerning the continuance or termination of corporate projects, as Statman and Tyebjee (1985) as well as Statman and Sepe (1989) exemplified in later studies.

In a seminal paper, Benartzi and Thaler (1995) combine the concept of loss aversion with the influence of different time horizon lengths in individual observation periods. Shorter, more frequent evaluation periods e.g. significantly alter investment decisions between stocks and bonds. This phenomenon that has been called "myopic loss aversion" was subsequently tested and verified in experimental studies such as Haigh and List (2006) and Thaler et al. (1997).

Thaler (1980) also mentions the psychological factor of regret as a powerful decision enabler that prevents individuals from the realization of actual losses in favor of maintaining assets at a paper or book loss instead. This phenomenon has been called endowment effect or divestiture aversion and implies the tendency to attribute a higher value to an asset once it has been acquired. A subsequent disposal of such an asset would therefore only be conducted if a higher purchase price than the one that had been paid to acquire the asset could be gained. The difference between these two prices has been labeled "willingness to pay (WTP)" and "willingness to accept (WTA)" and their substantial variation has been empirically supported by several experimental studies such as Carmon and Ariely (2000), Shogren et al. (1994) and Hanemann (1991).

The decision not to terminate certain projects, no matter whether they are loss-making and value-destructive or not of real use to the investor anymore, was further examined by Samuelson and Zeckhauser (1988). Contrary to traditional utility theory, they attributed a high degree of importance to the possibility of preserving the status quo in decision problems and explained this "status quo bias" with a number of possible reasons. While replicating prior choices can in some situations in fact be rational (e.g. because transaction costs to change the situation would be too high), there are also cognitive misperceptions and psychological commitment as possible causes. These reasons could either persist in a human need for consistency or, once again, in regret avoidance and the prevalence of sunk costs effects (Kahneman et al. (1991)).

Having dealt with the causes of loss aversion, it is also important to point out the consequences of this behavioral pattern. One of the most important implications that have been empirically detected in individual and managerial behavior is the occurrence of escalating commitment, i.e. the unwillingness to give up a once-chosen project even under bad circumstances or pessimistic future outlooks, as Brockner (1992) pointed out. Even though this pattern was identified by most participants that were holding on to a failing course of action for too long, they nevertheless did not alter their previous approach.

A striking consequence of this behavioral pattern is the fact that individuals would rather start to invest heavily into a distressed project than to terminate it in a timely manner instead (Shefrin and Statman (1985)). This effect has been frequently called "throwing good money after bad" or, in an attempt to describe the human need to get even with a losing project with high personal involvement, "get-evenitis". An often-cited example for this phenomenon is US hardware company Apple Computer's pilot PDA project "Newton" that was not terminated for more than ten years although it generated significant losses for the company and was afflicted with serious technical problems Apple was never able to fully eliminate despite large investments (Shefrin (1999)).

Staw (1976) further conducted an experiment with 240 undergraduate business students to test the effects of escalating commitment in a hypothetical situation where the students had to choose between the financing of two projects. The results strongly confirmed the prevalence of escalating commitment in decision situations where the participants feel they have a high personal responsibility for a project's success. The allocation of resources to previously chosen losing projects was significantly higher in the test group with high personal responsibility than in the comparison group with low responsibility. This experiment substantiates the effects illustrated in the corporate example of Apple.

Besides these situations, there are also projects that are based on systematically biased project forecast estimates and managerial over-confidence (Gervais et al. (2001)). A wide-spread phenomenon among managers is hubris and the empire-building hypothesis that refers to the desire to operate larger companies. The reasons for this behavior might be obvious, since managers of large corporations are likely to receive higher compensation and more public attention. In order to increase company sizes, managers tend to participate excessively in the takeover market and in a variety of corporate projects that are associated with large investments (Heaton (2002)). In an illusion of control, these managers pay overpriced acquisition premiums and systematically alter project forecasts with elevated revenue and underrated cost estimations (Shefrin (2001)).

Other aspects of behavioral finance theory include mass psychology effects that affect individual behavior as depicted e.g. by Bikhchandani et al. (1998). Phenomena such as herding behavior have been known for a long time and can be exemplified by the observation of media hypes or stock market bubbles (Baker and Wurgler (2007)). The tendency to imitate the behavior of others seems to be in human nature and is also observed in investment decisions.

Scharfstein and Stein (1990) develop a model that is able to explain herding phenomena in individual behavior in the stock market as well as in corporate decision-making processes. Individuals also measure their own gains and losses relative to those of other market participants. In what is often called a "sharing-the-blame hypothesis", individual losses are perceived as less painful in situations of general economic distress (e.g. in stock market crashes) compared to losses suffered by an individual in a climate of an economic upswing.

Previous studies have identified and analyzed a wide array of psychological components influencing corporate decision-making processes and concluded that expected utility theory is not a realistic model of economic behavior (Rabin and Thaler (2001)). In the following, we will demonstrate how several of these aspects can be closely applied to the case of ESCADA AG's belated disposal of its non-core segment PRIMERA AG and its subsequent insolvency of 2009.

In the following chapter, we illustrate ESCADA's divestment process of PRIMERA AG in a distinctive three-phase pattern. For each of these phases, we point out the behavioral finance implications that can be observed in the behavior of the company's management and analyze how these psychological effects significantly biased the decision-making process to sell off the subsidiary and to focus on the company's core competencies instead.

4.3 BEHAVIORAL FINANCE AND THE PRIMERA DISPOSAL

4.3.1 Historical background of ESCADA (1976-2000)

ESCADA was founded in 1976 by German businessman Wolfgang Ley and his wife Margaretha with headquarters in Munich. Due to its strong positioning and unique fashion style with an emphasis on strong colors and baroque era resemblance, ESCADA quickly rose to the top of the luxury women's ready-to-wear market, also accoutering many international celebrities on prestigious occasions such as the Academy Awards. The company's success story led to its 1986 IPO on the Frankfurt Stock Exchange as well as the gathering of numerous fashion awards, e.g. the Dallas Fashion Award in 1987 and the European Fashion Diamond Award in 1989. The death of co-founder and creative director Margaretha Ley in 1992, however, marked a turning point in the company's history.

Under the leadership of CEO Wolfgang Ley and new creative director Brian Rennie, ESCADA focused on a growth and diversification strategy throughout the 1990s, establishing the business lines ESCADA Beaute (in 1990), ESCADA Sport (1994), ESCADA Eyewear (1998), ESCADA Accessories and ESCADA Diamond Jewelry Collection (both 2000). Some further acquisitions such as that of US knitwear manufacturer St. John (divested in 1993), German fashion house Kurt Neumann GmbH (divested in 1998) as well as US designer Badgley Mischka (sold to Iconix Brand Group in 2004) were rather negligible in terms of company size and significance within the ESCADA Group.

In 1987, however, ESCADA acquired Muenster-based Schneberger Textilvertriebs GmbH which specialized in mid-price segment women's ready-to-wear apparel and which would later be the basis for the company's non-core segment PRIMERA AG. The Schneberger brand was renamed cavita fashion GmbH in 1999. A second brand named apriori Textilvertriebsgesellschaft mbH was established as a fully-owned subsidiary of Schneberger in 1989. Duisburg-based BIBA Mode GmbH was acquired as a third brand for the PRIMERA universe in three steps over the course of the years 1998 to 2005. The fourth and last brand was Laurèl which was originally established by ESCADA as a more affordable fashion line alongside the ESCADA Collection flagship brand in the 1980s. The

Laurèl brand was spun-off as a judicially independent company in 2001 and subsequently integrated into PRIMERA AG in 2003.

Although all of PRIMERA's brands pursued individual business strategies and had slightly different target groups, they all shared some distinctive characteristics that set them apart from the group's core business segments. While ESCADA was an international luxury brand, the PRIMERA brands were mostly focused on the German and some adjacent European markets with their price levels classifying them as representatives of the upscale mid-price segment.

Furthermore, PRIMERA used a multi-channel distribution strategy including self- and franchise-operated shops, shop-in-shop corners and multi-brand retailers in many German cities whereas ESCADA products were mainly distributed via flagship shops and only a few carefully selected department stores in international metropolises. This positioning resulted in a complete lack of synergies between ESCADA and PRIMERA, a fact that was also confirmed by management during the structured disposal process at the end of 2008.

By the year 2000, ESCADA was an internationally diversified fashion company. While the firm's sales still rose by high one-digit to low two-digit numbers per year throughout the 1990s, the company's profitability started to deteriorate by the end of the decade. This marks the starting point for our further analysis. We will illustrate the development of ESCADA AG in the following years from 2000 until its bankruptcy in August 2009 as well as the PRIMERA divestment process in a three-phase pattern in the following chapters. Figure 4.1 shows the performance of ESCADA AG's stock and the corresponding CDAX.

Figure 4.1: Share price performance of ESCADA AG's common stock

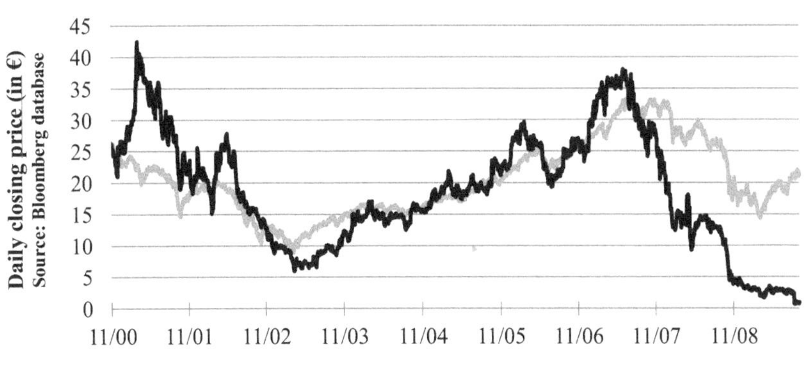

4.3.2 *Phase I (2000-2003)*

The beginning of the 21st century was characterized by a period of general economic distress due to the bursting of the dot-com bubble and the subsequent stock market crash. A series of macroeconomic events such as the SARS epidemic, the 9/11 US terror attacks as well as the wars in Afghanistan and Iraq triggered a strong downturn in international tourism and travel activity that had a strong impact on the luxury industry. ESCADA AG was also seriously affected by these events and fell into a state of crisis over the course of these years.

Table 4.1: ESCADA AG financials for FY2000/2001 to FY2002/2003[3]

COMPANY FINANCIALS (IN €M)	FISCAL YEAR 2000/2001	FISCAL YEAR 2001/2002	FISCAL YEAR 2002/2003
Total sales	846.2	772.9	620.8
Gross margin	*60.4%*	*61.3%*	*58.8%*
EBITDA	21.0	55.0	8.4
EBITDA margin	*2.5%*	*7.1%*	*1.4%*
EBIT	-17.1	25.1	-19.6
EBIT margin	*-2.0%*	*3.2%*	*(3.2%)*
Net profit / loss	-24.2	4.4	-77.7
Net debt	314.6	264.7	190.0
Equity ratio	*15.3%*	*17.0%*	*20.8%*

In fiscal year 2000/2001, the company reached a sales peak of €846.2m and employed more than 5,000 members of staff, both figures ESCADA was never able to exceed anymore. The company's profitability, however, hit a low point during this period, resulting in a net loss of €24.2m in the same year. Over the course of the next two years, sales fell drastically to €620.8m in fiscal year 2002/2003 when ESCADA suffered another fierce net loss of €77.7m. The company's stock mimicked its operational performance (see figure 4.1), falling by 86.0% from a peak of €42.40 on 6 March 2001 to €5.93 on 14 March 2003, underperforming the corresponding CDAX by -20.1%.

[3] All financial statement data on ESCADA AG and PRIMERA AG are taken from the respective quarterly and annual reports of ESCADA AG as published on the company's website, http://www.investor-relations.escada.com.

Following ESCADA's serious net loss of fiscal year 2000/2001, management and the supervisory board decided on a shift in direction away from the growth and diversification strategy that had been pursued throughout the 1990s. The new corporate refocusing strategy on ESCADA's core competencies in the luxury ladies' fashion segment was officially communicated to the public in the company's annual report of fiscal year 2000/2001, stating

> "In concurrence with the Supervisory Board, the Executive Board decided to concentrate ESCADA resources on the core business in the fiscal year 2000/2001. ESCADA AG therefore intends to sell interests in the Beauté Group (100%), in the Primera Group (90.1%), in the Laurèl business sector and an additional business sector. In addition, interests in the Kemper Group (90.1%) are to be transferred to the Féraud GmbH." [4]

In the following two years, ESCADA first sold its Beauté division to Darmstadt-based Wella Group in 2002 for an undisclosed amount. A long-term license agreement to produce and distribute cosmetic products and fragrances under the ESCADA brand label was negotiated by management. Secondly, the Kemper Group that included various business segments in the mid-price ladies' fashion sector (inter alia the manufacturing of womenswear under the well-known Cerruti 1881 label) was brought in to the Féraud GmbH, a joint venture between ESCADA and the Dutch Secon Group that had been established in 2001. The Féraud joint venture itself was subsequently divested to German investor Bavaria Modeholding AG in November 2003. The plan to divest itself of the remaining non-core segments was again emphasized in a statement from an ad hoc announcement dated from 4 June 2002:

> "As already announced, the ESCADA GROUP will continue to successively divest itself of its non-core businesses Laurèl, Kemper and Primera-Group. " [5]

The company's financial distress became increasingly threatening until fiscal year 2002/2003 when private equity investor HMD Capital Partners, a spin-off of Texas Pacific Group, acquired a 27% minority stake in ESCADA's equity for an amount of €45m. The proceeds from HMD's entrance via a capital increase were used for a reduction in the net debt position from €264.7m in fiscal year 2001/2002 down to €190.0m in fiscal year 2002/2003.

---

[4] ESCADA Group annual report for fiscal year 2000/2001, p. 138

[5] ESCADA Group ad hoc announcement from 4 June 2002 (as disclosed on http://www.investor-relations.escada.com)

By this means, ESCADA was saved for once from its downward spiral and was able to concentrate its activities on the implementation of both a cost-reduction as well as an efficiency program for its financial and operational re-structuring strategy. The decision to divest itself of its remaining non-core segments, namely PRIMERA AG and the then-stand-alone Laurèl GmbH, however, was put on hold for the time being in the wake of HMD's entrance. In its annual report for fiscal year 2002/2003, management announced:

> "The weakness of the textile markets and the adverse environment for M&A transactions slowed the progress of the project, inaugurated the year before, to divest all activities not belonging to the ESCADA brand: the Féraud Group, the Primera Group and the Laurèl Group." [6]

Laurèl GmbH was consolidated with PRIMERA AG in November 2003 in order to realize the potential of the promised synergies between the Laurèl brand and PRIMERA's existing portfolio of mid-price ladies' fashion brands that at the time included apriori, BiBA and cavita. While no officially disclosed measures for the initiation of a structured disposal process were published, management at this point still publicly insisted on its willingness to sell off the PRIMERA business after its future turnaround and return to profitability:

> "Even though the PRIMERA Group will remain part of the ESCADA Group for the time being, ESCADA is still holding firm to its goal of focusing entirely on the ESCADA brand within the medium term." [7]

Table 4.2: PRIMERA AG financials for FY2000/2001 to FY2002/2003

COMPANY FINANCIALS (IN €M)	FISCAL YEAR 2000/2001	FISCAL YEAR 2001/2002	FISCAL YEAR 2002/2003
Total sales	207.6	209.5	200.6
EBITDA	n.d.	5.2	-4.6
EBITDA margin	*n.d.*	*2.5%*	*-2.3%*
EBIT	-2.8	2.8	-10.6
EBIT margin	*-1.3%*	*1.3%*	*-5.3%*
Net profit / loss	-5.3	-2.0	-17.9
ESCADA Group total capex	42.8	22.5	22.6
thereof: PRIMERA AG	7.1	5.4	4.0

---

[6] ESCADA Group annual report for fiscal year 2002/2003, p. 131

[7] ESCADA Group annual report for fiscal year 2002/2003, p. 33

In fiscal year 2002/2003, PRIMERA reported sales of €200.6m and accounted for 32.3% of ESCADA Group's total sales volume. It suffered a severe net loss of €17.9m after having incurred further net losses in the two preceding fiscal years (see table 4.2). This marks a starting point for behavioral finance-based explanations of failed divestment decisions in the case of PRIMERA. It has been shown empirically that losses that were preceded by previous losses are considerably more painful than losses following prior gains.

This loss aversion shows parallels to Apple's Newton project. The human tendency to evaluate decision situations considering previous events rather than on a stand-alone basis becomes obvious (Barberis and Huang (2001)). Since ESCADA as well as PRIMERA suffered a series of net losses during the period of 2000 until 2003, only low purchase prices for PRIMERA could have been expected. This would have inflicted further losses upon the group and shows that the disposal hesitation is in line with the according literature.

Furthermore, it is a well-established phenomenon in behavioral finance that foregone gains are more likely to be accepted in a decision situation than actually realized losses. This is one possible explanation for the divestment hesitation during ESCADA's period of financial distress. In addition, the justification of the disposal deferral concerning the "adverse environment for M&A transactions" signals a difference between the potential buyers' willingness to pay and ESCADA management's willingness to accept for the first time.

This reason for the delay of the PRIMERA disposal has been stated repeatedly by management in official publications as can be seen in the following. It becomes evident that management and especially founder Wolfgang Ley have become personally involved with the PRIMERA segment over the course of its existence. We can therefore observe the difference between WTP and WTA in the case of ESCADA by looking at the redundant claim for an adequate purchase price for the PRIMERA segment by management.

4.3.3 Phase II (2003-2007)

Following HMD's entrance, ESCADA started a phase of partially successful corporate restructuring which was accompanied by a general upswing in the economy and the stock markets. The consumption climate in general as well as in the luxury fashion markets started to catch up, also due to a strong increase in international tourism and travel activity. Stock markets finally regained strength after the crash of 2000 until they reached all-time peaks in 2007.

During this time period, management implemented a rigorous efficiency and cost-cutting program that included the closing of unprofitable stores and the lay-offs of about 850 employees. Table 4.3 shows that a steady, though not competitive sales growth was achieved until the company reached sales of €695.2m in fiscal year 2005/2006 (CAGR of 3.9% starting from fiscal year 2002/2003). ESCADA's profitability started to slowly increase as well, resulting in EBITDA of €74.1m (10.7% of sales) and EBIT of €52.9m (7.6% of sales) in the same fiscal year. These years were also characterized by a series of three consecutive net profits as well as a reduction of net debt and increased equity ratio.

Table 4.3: ESCADA AG financials for FY2003/2004 to FY2005/2006

COMPANY FINANCIALS (IN €M)	FISCAL YEAR 2003/2004	FISCAL YEAR 2004/2005	FISCAL YEAR 2005/2006
Total sales	625.5	648.6	695.2
Gross margin	*60.6%*	*62.8%*	*62.4%*
EBITDA	47.3	65.1	74.1
EBITDA margin	*7.6%*	*10.0%*	*10.7%*
EBIT	25.2	45.6	52.9
EBIT margin	*4.0%*	*7.0%*	*7.6%*
Net profit / loss	3.8	13.7	6.9
Net debt	208.7	207.7	188.7
Equity ratio	*20.0%*	*23.5%*	*26.4%*

ESCADA AG's stock price performance during this second period was able to benefit both from the general upswing in international stock markets and the company's own return to profitability. In the course of these favorable conditions, the stock price reached a peak of €38.00 on 1 June 2007. Over the course of this period (starting with HMD's entrance on 30 June 2003 and ending with the dismissal of CEO Frank Rheinboldt on 30 May 2007), ESCADA's stock even outperformed the also-recovering CDAX by a considerable 196.8%.

While the restructuring measures implemented by ESCADA management had positive implications for the company and led to a series of proper results, a number of new issues nevertheless paved the way for the company's impending next crisis. First troubles arose with the acquisition of HMD by Swiss-based investor group Finartis and its main shareholder Rustam Aksenenko. His operational interference and ongoing controversies about ESCADA's strategy led to a wave of personnel changes in top management positions.

First, CFO Georg Kellinghusen resigned on 31 December 2005 and was succeeded by former member of the supervisory board Marcus Schuerholz. Only one month later, ESCADA founder Wolfgang Ley stepped down from his post as CEO on 31 January 2006 and was succeeded by Frank Rheinboldt, another former member of the supervisory board. Being dissatisfied with Rheinboldt, however, Aksenenko replaced him only 16 months later with former LVMH vice president Jean-Marc Loubier. In addition, creative director Brian Rennie was succeeded by Damiano Biella. Finally, Loubier was also replaced by Bruno Saelzer, the former CEO of Hugo Boss AG in July 2008.

The different management teams tried to implement a new business strategy and a restructuring program, but were not able to eliminate some of ESCADA's key operating issues. The first was the company's continuously weak performance in the important leather accessories collection which made up for less than 10.0% of total ESCADA sales throughout the entire decade whereas peer group firms such as Hermès International and Louis Vuitton generated a lion's share of their total sales volume with highly profitable accessories collections.

Another major operating issue ESCADA management had to face during this period was the company's completely unstructured sales and distribution strategy. Sales density was reported at a disastrous €7,000/m^2 in fiscal year 2006/2007 while Hermès International and Louis Vuitton reached well above €30,000/m^2 during the same period in time. Furthermore, there were no clearly defined corporate guidelines for the choice of both the locations of new store openings as well as adequate sales floor sizes. These issues were addressed as top priority measures in a restructuring program called "ESCADA Excellence" that was implemented in June 2007 by CEO Jean-Marc Loubier.

Table 4.4: PRIMERA AG financials for FY2003/2004 to FY2005/2006

COMPANY FINANCIALS (IN €M)	FISCAL YEAR 2003/2004	FISCAL YEAR 2004/2005	FISCAL YEAR 2005/2006
Total sales	205.8	211.5	227.4
EBITDA	13.3	18.1	20.1
EBITDA margin	*6.5%*	*8.6%*	*8.8%*
EBIT	8.7	13.9	15.6
EBIT margin	*4.2%*	*6.6%*	*6.9%*
Net profit / loss	9.1	5.0	8.0
ESCADA Group total capex	18.6	21.5	31.3
thereof: PRIMERA AG	2.0	4.7	7.5

In line with ESCADA's positive sales and earnings development, PRIMERA's operational performance also started to improve significantly. From fiscal year 2002/2003 to 2006/2007, sales increased by a CAGR of 5.4% from €200.6m to €247.7m. Net profits were generated throughout these years while EBITDA and EBIT margins caught up to solid levels of 8-9% and 6-7%, respectively. Capital expenditures in the amount of €22.8m were invested in the non-core segment during this period that were mainly used for the improvement of PRIMERA's retail network, especially for the BiBA and Laurèl brands (including both the refurbishment of existing as well as the opening of new stores).

Further investments were made for the IT infrastructure used in the retail network and the purchase of concessions. Since these were mostly investments for operational improvements, it appears that management tried to achieve a successful turnaround of PRIMERA and to get even with its non-core segment. The phenomenon of "get-evenitis" that is well-known in behavioral finance literature is therefore well applicable in this case. Nevertheless, it will become even more obvious in the subsequent fiscal years when management increased the magnitude of capital expenditures in the PRIMERA segment even further.

While ESCADA ostensibly insisted on its willingness to pursue the divestiture plans for PRIMERA after its imminent return to profitability, it can be noted from various statements in annual reports and ad hoc announcements that management yet gradually dismissed these plans over the course of this second phase. While the core brand ESCADA and the PRIMERA business were still distinctively differentiated as two independent segments throughout ESCADA Group's annual reports and ad hoc announcements and PRIMERA was sometimes only referred to as a "successful financial investment"[8], there were also a lot of indications that management would completely abandon the intended disposal plan. For example, CEO Frank Rheinboldt quoted:

> "The PRIMERA Group will also continue its course and gradually position itself as vertical provider in the premium and mid-price segment with a strong international focus." [9]

Further hints for the dismissal of the divestiture process included references to PRIMERA's successful turnaround and its strong contribution to ESCADA Group's sales and earnings growth during these years:

---

[8] ESCADA Group annual report for fiscal year 2006/2007, p. 8

[9] ESCADA Group annual report for fiscal year 2005/2006, p. 10

"According to the final figures of the Group's Annual Financial Statement now available, Group sales were up by 3.7% to EUR 648.6 million (vs. EUR 625.5 million in 2003/2004). Currency adjusted the plus comes to 4.3%. Both business areas, ESCADA as well as the PRIMERA Group, contributed toward this growth." [10]

Figure 4.2: EV/EBITDA multiple valuation of PRIMERA AG

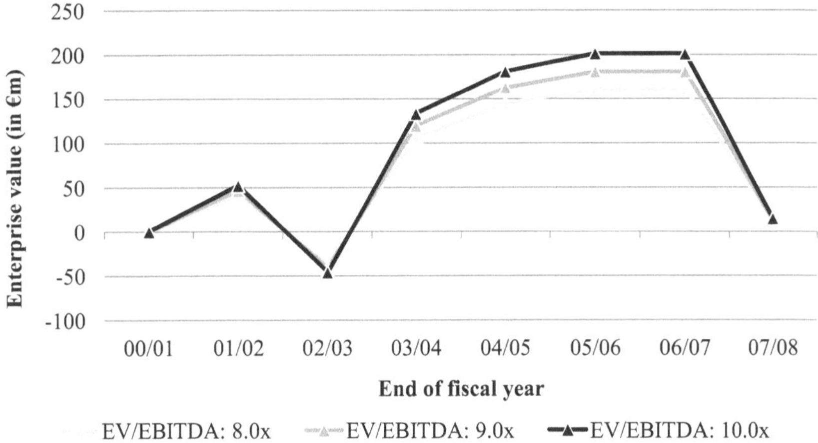

During this second phase of the intended divestiture process, the implied value of the business segment started to increase due to PRIMERA's good operational performance, its sales growth and the net profits it generated. Figures 4.2 and 4.3 illustrate the implied enterprise value development of the PRIMERA segment using industry average EV/EBITDA and EV/EBIT multiples[11].

After three fiscal years of small or even negative valuations, PRIMERA's implied enterprise value sharply increased during the phase from fiscal year 2003/2004 until it peaked in fiscal year 2006/2007 when reaching consistent values between €150m and €200m. This implied value range had also been confirmed independently by numerous broker reports on ESCADA AG, some of which were also based on more detailed and insightful DCF valuation methodologies that were applied to the PRIMERA business segment.

---

[10] ESCADA Group ad hoc announcement from 3 March 2006 (as disclosed on http://www.investor-relations.escada.com)

[11] Industry average EV/EBITDA and EV/EBIT multiples have been taken from broker reports on ESCADA AG as well as the fashion market in general by Aurel Leven, Bankhaus Lampe, Berenberg Bank, Deutsche Bank, DZ Bank, HVB/UniCredit and Sal. Oppenheim.

Figure 4.3: EV/EBIT multiple valuation of PRIMERA AG

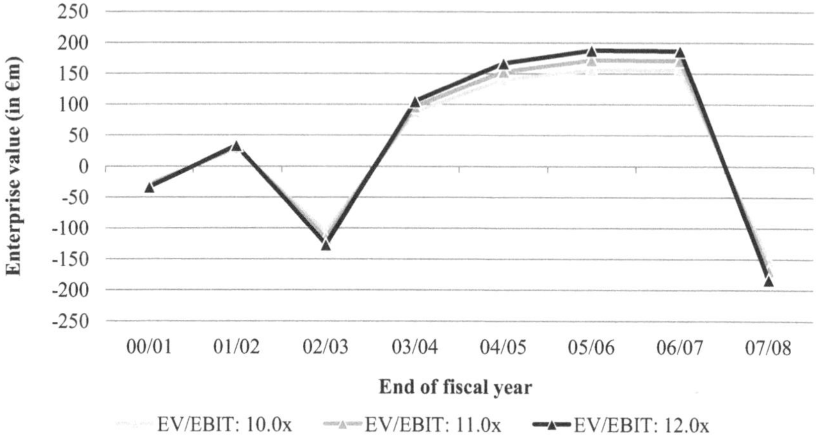

The implied enterprise values represent a significant proportion of ESCADA's net debt position throughout these years, while in fiscal years 2005/2006 and 2006/2007 they would have even exceeded it by up to €36.4m. From a purchase price-oriented point of view, these years can therefore be viewed as an optimal time window for the long-intended disposal of the PRIMERA business. Net proceeds in the amount discussed before would have helped ESCADA significantly to strengthen its balance sheet, restructure its core brands as well as the weak accessories collection and to cover up almost its entire indebtedness.

While it has been rumored by financial analysts and the media that ESCADA never received an appropriate and genuine offer bid for its PRIMERA business, the virtually non-existent public communication about the proceedings of the disposal process leads us to the conclusion that management did in fact not actively pursue divestiture negotiations during this period at all.

Instead of pursuing the PRIMERA AG divestment despite the perspective of lucrative purchase prices, ESCADA further adhered to the subsidiary. In March 2005, the company issued a €200m junk bond with seven-year maturity, a 7.5% coupon payment and a credit rating of BB-/B2 as well as a €90m syndicated loan for refinancing matters instead. This is another clear indication of the strong disposal hesitation of ESCADA's management.

In behavioral finance, regret is assumed to be one of the most powerful emotions concerning the decision of project terminations or divestiture activities. In an ex ante examination, management would have had to admit its own shortcomings in the restructuring process of PRIMERA if they had sold the business segment before its return to profitability. This assumption would certainly apply to the first phase of fiscal years 2000/2001 until 2002/2003 when PRIMERA incurred net losses and sales volumes were decreasing.

A second way in which regret influences divestiture decisions derives from an ex post point of view. In the case of an accomplished disposal, the further development of PRIMERA under new ownership would still have been easily observable for ESCADA in the market. This way, regret would have resulted from the achievement of a successful turnaround initiated by the new owners. This fact would apply to fiscal years 2003/2004 until 2006/2007 when PRIMERA started to generate small net profits and sales growth again. The unwillingness to accept its own incapability to restructure PRIMERA therefore seems to be one of the most important causes of management's divestiture aversion.

Another explanation for management's disposal hesitation that applies especially to this second period of 2003 to 2007 is herding behavior. While a disposal of PRIMERA during these years presumably would have supplied the group with sufficient liquidity for a successful restructuring of its core brand, it would also have significantly decreased ESCADA Group's company size in terms of both sales and employees. As we already pointed out, managers tend to prefer large companies to small ones due to higher compensation and public attention which is described by the empire-building hypothesis. PRIMERA accounted for roughly one third of ESCADA's total sales over the course of this second phase, a disposal therefore would have considerably reduced the company's revenue basis as well as its portfolio of different business lines.

A divestment would have been a rather unusual step in an industry where the dominant and successful companies such as Hermès International, LVMH and PPR are large in scale as well as diversified in their product portfolios. It would also have made ESCADA an easier takeover target in a market segment of high consolidation. Management's conviction that PRIMERA could be successfully restructured and be held as a strong second foothold (as indicated by the statements cited above) can therefore be seen as a sign of newly-found (over-) confidence in a period of improving operational performance.

4.3.4 Phase III (2007-2009)

The third and last phase of ESCADA's development is characterized by the worldwide financial crisis with its beginning in the sub-prime mortgage crisis of

2007. The international stock markets in general and the highly sensitive luxury fashion markets in particular were also heavily affected by these macroeconomic developments, starting with the year 2008. Due to its prevailing operational and strategic issues, these external events significantly intensified ESCADA's worsening situation and also played an important role in the company's declaration of bankruptcy in August 2009.

Table 4.5: ESCADA AG financials for FY2006/2007 to Q2 2008/2009

COMPANY FINANCIALS (IN €M)	FISCAL YEAR 2006/2007	FISCAL YEAR 2007/2008	Q2 OF FISCAL YEAR 2008/2009
Total sales	686.1	582.1	248.1
Gross margin	*63.4%*	*63.6%*	*64.4%*
EBITDA	68.2	19.5	2.2
EBITDA margin	*9.9%*	*3.3%*	*0.9%*
EBIT	47.1	-23.7	-8.1
EBIT margin	*6.9%*	*-4.1%*	*-3.3%*
Net profit / loss	-27.3	-70.3	-91.7
Net debt	164.7	177.1	187.6
Equity ratio	*19.5%*	*17.5%*	*-5.2%*

While the luxury goods markets were still booming in ESCADA's fiscal year 2006/2007, the company was not able to participate in this positive development due to unusually high one-time expenses attributed to restructuring measures of the "ESCADA Excellence" program. Sales fell only slightly by 1.3% down to €686.1m, but the group suffered a net loss of €27.3m. In fiscal year 2007/2008, the situation went from bad to worse due to the impending financial crisis and sales fell drastically to €582.1m with a corresponding net loss in the amount of €70.3m. Net debt which had been reduced constantly over the course of the preceding years due to high free cash flow levels increased again from €164.7m to €177.1m. In the second quarterly report of fiscal year 2008/2009 (the last one that was disclosed prior to the company's insolvency), ESCADA had already accumulated a negative EBIT of €8.1m and a net loss of €91.7m.

The company's downward spiral and the general downturn in the economy were also echoed by the performance of ESCADA's stock that incurred a steep decline in value. Share prices fell down to €0.70 on 13 August 2009 when the company's bankruptcy was publicly announced, representing a 98.1% loss compared to the price of €37.70 at which the stock was trading on 31 May 2007, the day after Frank Rheinboldt's replacement by Jean-Marc Loubier as CEO was announced. Despite the strong underperformance of ESCADA's stock compared to the CDAX of -63.4%, no public takeover bid was made for the company which indicates a weak market for corporate control in Germany.

The operational and strategic improvements that were promised by the "ESCADA Excellence" program were moderate at best and did not strengthen the company's performance. In addition, the first collections of new creative director Damiano Biella failed to attract the old customer basis due to his use of unusually dark colors and slimmer dress cuts, resulting in sharply declining pre-collection orders. The constant wave of personnel changes led shareholders, employees and other stakeholders to lose faith in the company. Private equity investor Apax Partners, for example, dismissed its participation interest in ESCADA due to the company's weak share price performance in April 2008.[12]

In June 2008, the wealthy German Herz brothers Wolfgang and Michael each acquired a 12.45% stake in the group via a capital increase to strengthen the company's equity capital base. The proceeds were used mainly for the refinancing of the €90m syndicated loan granted to ESCADA in 2005 whereas the repayment of the principal for the outstanding €200m notes due in 2012 became increasingly threatening. In June 2009, a bond exchange offer was issued in which bondholders would have had to agree on a 60% value write-off in exchange for two kinds of newly-issued notes and a small cash payment.

Most likely in anticipation of better conditions, the bondholders' majority rejected the exchange offer even after a slight amendment was handed in one month later. As a consequence, ESCADA's board of directors filed for insolvency on 13 August 2009. On 5 November 2009, ESCADA was acquired by a trust held by Indian steel magnate's daughter Megha Mittal and is supposed to pursuit its previous strategy implemented by CEO Dr. Bruno Saelzer since.

PRIMERA's performance differed from ESCADA's during this last period. While ESCADA sales decreased in fiscal year 2006/2007, PRIMERA generated a sales growth of 8.9% up to €247.7m. With an EBITDA of €20.1m (8.1% of sales), an EBIT of €15.6m (6.3% of sales) and a net profit of €9.5m (3.8% of sales), the subsidiary achieved a strong result. Since ESCADA was already facing financial distress, a divestment would have made all the more sense given PRIMERA's implied enterprise value of between €150m and €200m at the time

---

[12] ESCADA Group ad hoc announcement from 9 April 2008 (as disclosed on http://www.investor-relations.escada.com)

(see figures 4.2 and 4.3). Not until fiscal year 2007/2008, PRIMERA's performance started to deteriorate as total sales fell by -14.8% down to €211.0m.

Table 4.6: PRIMERA AG financials for FY2006/2007 to Q2 2008/2009

COMPANY FINANCIALS (IN €M)	FISCAL YEAR 2006/2007	FISCAL YEAR 2007/2008	Q2 OF FISCAL YEAR 2008/2009
Total sales	247.7	211.0	98.9
EBITDA	20.1	1.5	-12.8
EBITDA margin	*8.1%*	*0.7%*	*-12.9%*
EBIT	15.6	-15.2	-16.2
EBIT margin	*6.3%*	*-7.2%*	*-16.4%*
Net profit / loss	9.5	n.d.	-73.9
ESCADA Group total capex	33.8	35.4	12.7
thereof: PRIMERA AG	4.6	9.6	8.7

Following a profit warning in June 2008 which was mainly attributed to the "poor performance" of the "business-sensitive fast fashion segment of the PRIMERA brands" [13], management finally started to concentrate again on its disposal considerations for the PRIMERA business segment. The official start of the structured divestiture process was disclosed on 5 December 2008 via an ad hoc announcement in which management also declared:

> "There are no synergies with the core business of the ESCADA brand." [14]

Three days later management released yet another ad hoc announcement that was a direct response to a critical article that had previously been published in the weekly German periodical "Focus". In this article, the editors had speculated about a connection between the announced disposal plans and the company's financial troubles. The ad hoc announcement said:

> "The fact that ESCADA announced last Friday that the process of selling its subsidiary PRIMERA AG is starting now has nothing to do with alleged liquidity problems but constitutes a principal decision of company strategy. This step has been preceded by extensive consultations in the Management and Supervisory Board,

[13] ESCADA Group ad hoc announcement from 20 June 2008 (as disclosed on http://www.investor-relations.escada.com)

[14] ESCADA Group ad hoc announcement from 5 December 2008 (as disclosed on http://www.investor-relations.escada.com)

reaching back as far as the year 2007. To term this a "hasty sale" as the "Focus" does is therefore incorrect." [15]

Although the structured divestiture process had now been started, management still hesitated to quickly follow through with the disposal as can be observed by a quotation from the annual report of fiscal year 2007/2008:

"If it proves to be impossible to obtain an adequate sales price in line with market conditions, the earnings situation of ESCADA Group and ESCADA AG could be further adversely affected. Alternatively, it cannot be ruled out that the Board of Management should decide not to sell the subsidiary or not at the present time." [16]

PRIMERA was then finally sold off in two transactions in May and June 2009, respectively. While Munich-based German private equity investor mutares AG took over the apriori, cavita and Laurèl brands (announced on 26 May 2009), German ladies' fashion house GELCO GmbH & Co.KG with headquarters in Gelsenkirchen acquired the remaining BiBA brand which was announced on 5 June 2009. Once again, ESCADA management publicly insisted:

"The divesture is a key element in the Group's ongoing strategic reorientation and financial restructuring." [17]

While purchase prices have not been disclosed in both M&A transaction announcements, the quarterly financial report for the first half of ESCADA AG's fiscal year 2008/2009 reported net proceeds from the divestiture of the PRIMERA business in the amount of €10m. This amount represents less than 10% of the enterprise value estimations for PRIMERA during the period of fiscal years 2004/2005 to 2006/2007 (see figures 4.2 and 4.3).

Considering the fact that the capital expenditures spent on the PRIMERA business in the first half of fiscal year 2008/2009, i.e. right before the divestiture of the non-core segment amounted to €8.7m, there were basically no positive proceeds from the disposal at all that could have been used for the financial restructuring of ESCADA. We therefore conclude that the optimal timing choice for a disposal of PRIMERA has been clearly missed by management.

---

[15] ESCADA Group ad hoc announcement from 8 December 2008 (as disclosed on http://www.investor-relations.escada.com)

[16] ESCADA Group annual report for fiscal year 2007/2008, p. 82

[17] ESCADA Group ad hoc announcement from 26 May 2009 (as disclosed on http://www.investor-relations.escada.com)

Over the course of fiscal year 2006/2007 to the first half of fiscal year 2008/2009, ESCADA management invested another considerable amount of €22.9m in the PRIMERA business segment. The phenomenon of "get-evenitis" that we had already identified throughout the second phase becomes even more evident in this period when PRIMERA's performance also started to deteriorate. It can be said that management threw good money after bad in its struggle to return the non-core segment to profitability by all means necessary.

This kind of escalating commitment can be further explained by the sunk costs effect which was also observable in the Apple Newton case. Since ESCA-DA invested a total of €53.6m in the PRIMERA business over the course of the decade, it becomes abundantly clear that management wanted to retrieve these foregone gains via a disposal which is illogical by the methodology of NPV project valuation techniques that correctly do not factor in sunk costs, but only future cash flows. The claim for an "adequate purchase price" for PRIMERA that was made again immediately preceding ESCADA's bankruptcy underlines management's strong unwillingness to give up the subsidiary without being able to retrieve the money invested in it over the course of the previous years.

Finally, we also view this behavioral pattern as a strong form of a prevailing status quo bias, since it appears that management did not see sufficient incentives to change the predominant situation with PRIMERA as a second business line. The illusion of being able to attain a high acquisition premium for a disposal of PRIMERA prevented management to settle for a realistic purchase price at a fair value even during the second period when a considerable monetary amount of between €150m and €200m could have been received.

Management, however, insisted on its own (overly optimistic) price range that was subjectively altered by the inclusion of sunk costs due to high investments and the personal feeling of responsibility for the non-core segment by management. Therefore, retaining the status quo, even though PRIMERA started to incur losses in the end as well, was perceived as less painful than realizing actual losses via a disposal for a seemingly inadequate purchase price.

4.4 CONCLUSION

Given its complete lack of synergies with ESCADA AG's main business activities in the luxury fashion industry as well as its implied value range of up to €200m in fiscal year 2006/2007, a disposal of the non-core segment PRIMERA AG at the optimal point in time would have been an important and reasonable decision to focus on ESCADA's core business. The proceedings from a divestiture would have endowed the company with enough liquidity to significantly strengthen its balance sheet and refinance its outstanding debt.

Furthermore, it would have given ESCADA sufficient financial headroom for important restructuring measures such as the implementation of new sales and distribution strategies as well as an improvement of the accessories business line. Despite the undeniable advantages of a disposal, management apparently suffered from a strong case of loss aversion and status quo bias and deferred the long-anticipated divestiture of PRIMERA for almost an entire decade.

This clinical paper represents a practical exemplification of the importance that psychological effects can exert on corporate decision-making processes. It illustrates that a company's management can get seriously entrapped with losing projects, especially in case these projects include a high degree of personal involvement and responsibility. As the example of ESCADA AG illustrates, these effects can lead to the deferral of project termination decisions up until the point where they seriously endanger a company's survival. With its new owners in charge and only its core brand left after emerging from the insolvency proceedings, ESCADA now has the opportunity to alter its approach and to regain its position among the world's leading brands in the luxury fashion market.

As far as divestiture activities in the fashion and accessories industry are concerned on a more general level, we also conclude that the disposal of a subsidiary or portfolio brand can in fact be advantageous for their parent companies. While PRIMERA did not share any synergies with ESCADA's core business segment, it well increased complexity and bound capacities in the firm's organization. A refocusing on a company's core competencies can therefore be an important measure for the improvement of corporate efficiency and profitability that should not be limited to situations of financial distress.

5 LONG-RUN PERFORMANCE AND RISK CHANGES FOLLOWING FASHION IPOS

5.1 INTRODUCTION

The fashion and leather accessories industry exhibits a very heterogeneous business structure. On one hand, a few large, internationally diversified conglomerates such as LVMH, Phillips-Van Heusen and PPR regularly add further brands to their portfolios and steadily increase company sizes. On the other hand, there are still many fashion houses such as Lanvin, Roberto Cavalli and Versace that are still rather modest-scale, single-brand businesses. For these smaller companies it is not uncommon to be closely connected and publicly associated with central personalities such as their founder or present creative director.

This heterogeneity of the fashion industry is also apparent in firms' ownership structures. While most of the large firms have been publicly listed for many years, some founders of smaller, private fashion companies such as Jil Sander, Valentino Garavani and Wolfgang Joop have sold their businesses to financial sponsors or strategic investors as an exit strategy. Mergers and acquisitions, however, are not the only option for change of control processes. In this paper, we will instead analyze the determinants of the long-run stock price performance of initial public offerings in the fashion and accessories industry.

The industry has seen a considerable number of high-profile IPOs that were conducted on foreign stock exchanges, the most recent of which being Italian luxury house Prada's $2.1bn offering in June 2011 on the Hong Kong Stock Exchange. Further examples include Esprit Holdings that was also initially listed in Hong Kong and the intended European IPO of US apparel manufacturer Tommy Hilfiger that was finally withdrawn by owners Apax Partners. This is a rather unusual finding, since many empirical studies such as Hartmann et al. (2007) find that foreign issuers significantly underperform domestic offerings.

In order to give a more conclusive overview of fashion IPOs, we use a data sample comprising 207 international equity offerings conducted between 1990 and 2007. We analyze deal characteristics such as issuing company geographies and financials, initial underpricing and the long-run stock price performance for three years following these IPOs. We further conduct cross-sectional regression analysis to identify the key drivers of post-IPO stock price performance. Finally, we also analyze shifts in fashion company betas in order to control for systematic risk changes following initial public offerings.

The paper proceeds as follows. Section 5.2 gives an overview of previous research conducted in the field of initial public offerings. It focuses mainly on the going-public decision process, initial underpricing as well as the long-run underperformance of IPO companies. Section 5.3 illustrates the data and methodology used in our analysis. Section 5.4 presents the results of our long-term event study as well as our cross-sectional regression and changes in systematic risk analyses. Section 5.5 summarizes our findings and concludes.

5.2 LITERATURE OVERVIEW

The initial public offering of a company's equity represents a major corporate event and has been extensively researched throughout the corporate finance literature. A recent comprehensive review of various IPO-related research issues is given in Eckbo et al. (2007) and Ritter (2003). Theoretical models for the decision to go public have been discussed by Fischer (2000) and Chemmanur and Fulghieri (1999) while Pagano et al. (1998) show empirical determinants of the going-public decision using a unique data set of Italian issuing companies. They identify company sizes and market-to-book ratios as two of these key determinants and also find a significant drop in cost of credit following an IPO. They conclude that this is mostly due to higher bargaining power of public firms in bank negotiations. Ang and Boyer (2009) further use the aftermath of the 1987 stock market crash as an example for the cyclical variability in IPO activity.

The major part of the existing IPO literature, however, has rather focused on two phenomena that have been reported in many empirical studies: Short-term underpricing and long-term underperformance. Underpricing constitutes the percental difference between a security's offer price and its first closing price in the secondary market. Since these price differences represent foregone gains to the issuing company, underpricing is also commonly referred to as "money left on the table". One of the first studies that have illustrated the extent of IPO underpricing was Ibbotson (1975) who reported an average price jump of 11.4% for a sample of 2,650 US IPOs between 1960 and 1969.

In the following decades, countless papers have analyzed the amount of underpricing in various industries and different time periods. Extensive surveys of changes in underpricing over time are given by Dolvin and Pyles (2007) and Loughran and Ritter (2004). Further research has also focused on the influence of institutional frameworks on initial IPO performance. The positive role venture capital companies play in the creation of public companies has been analyzed e.g. by Bessler and Kurth (2007), Megginson and Weiss (1991) and Barry et al. (1990), while Cooney et al. (2001) report a negative relationship between underwriter reputation and IPO underpricing. Jain and Martin (2005) find similar results for the impact of audit quality on IPO performance.

Various studies have also concentrated on the theoretical explanation of this phenomenon. Rock (1986) attributes IPO underpricing to asymmetrically informed investors ("lemon's market"). This model has been advanced by Benveniste and Spindt (1989) and Beatty and Ritter (1986). Further theories try to explain underpricing as a means to create attractiveness to potential SEO investors (Welch (1989)) or to avoid possible lawsuits (Lowry and Shu (2002)).

Newer approaches rather focus on behavioral finance arguments such as mental accounting and point out that managers are indifferent towards leaving money on the table since they are well-compensated as shareholders of the company by the price jump in the secondary market (Loughran and Ritter (2002)). Other than that, underpricing could also be attributed to conflicts of interest when underwriters either promise favorable analyst coverage to the issuing firm (Dhiensiri and Sayrak (2010)) or allocate deliberately underpriced shares in order to gain future investment banking business (Loughran and Ritter (2004)).

Despite this unusually positive performance in the first days of public trading, a lot of research has shown empirically that IPO shares significantly underperform the market in the long-run. In one of the first studies, Ritter (1991) analyzes a set of 1,526 US IPOs during 1975 to 1984 and finds that these shares underperform those of matching firms by 17% over a three-year buy-and-hold period. Many others such as Brav et al. (2000) document that underperformance is particularly driven by small growth stocks as well as non-venture capital-backed IPOs. Chang et al. (2010) and Carter et al. (1998) again report a positive influence of underwriter reputation on the long-run stock price performance. While long-term underperformance is also commonly attributed to asymmetrically distributed information and investor sentiment, a more conclusive explanation of this phenomenon is rarely given in the empirical studies cited above.

An often-cited explanation of long-term IPO underperformance is given by Eckbo and Norli (2005). They argue that IPOs do indeed yield generally low returns, but also have lower risk exposures and show empirically that IPO companies have higher stock turnover as well as lower leverage which should result in lower systematic risk. This approach is developed further by Carlson et al. (2004, 2006) who use a real options framework to explain that firms commonly use the proceeds of a seasoned equity offering to exercise real options such as acquiring another company or investing in a corporate project. These investments should turn risky growth opportunities into lower-risk assets in place and thereby lower the company's beta. In a later study, Carlson et al. (2010) empirically show that systematic risk of issuing companies indeed gradually decreases in the three post-SEO years.

According to this theory that was advanced inter alia by Cooper and Priestley (2011), low offer returns are not caused by systematic mispricing or investor sentiment, but a general reduction in systematic risk. We believe fashion companies to be particularly subject to a high risk exposure due to their strong dependence on mostly two annual collections' appreciation by customers. Using the proceeds from an equity offering to build or acquire additional brands and diversifying their revenue streams should therefore result in a general risk reduction. While Carlson et al. (2006, 2010) focus solely on seasoned equity offerings, they also suggest that the implications of their model should apply to IPOs as well. We therefore conduct an analysis of changes in company betas following fashion and accessories offerings in section 5.4.

5.3 DATA AND METHODOLOGY

5.3.1 Data

We identify fashion and leather accessories initial public offerings using the SDC/Thomson One Banker Deals database. In order to be included in the data sample, the respective transactions have to meet the following criteria:

(1) The transaction is denominated as an initial public offering (IPO flag).

(2) The issuing company has a primary two-digit SIC code within the major groups "23 – Apparel and Other Finished Products Made From Fabrics And Similar Materials" or "56 – Apparel and Accessory Stores".

(3) The issuance date is between 1 January 1990 and 31 December 2007.

(4) The transaction was not withdrawn and liquid monthly trading data for the 36 months following the IPO are available on the Thomson Financial Datastream database.

Criterion (1) ensures that only initial public offerings of common stock are considered and subsequent offerings such as SEOs are excluded. Industry affiliation is applied by using the major two-digit SIC code groups for apparel manufacturers (group "23") as well as retailers (group "56"), hence criterion (2). Criterion (3) determines that monthly stock data for three full trading years (36 months) has to be available. Since IPO activity sharply declined in the wake of the worldwide financial crisis of 2008, this does not exclude a large number of deals. The first noteworthy fashion IPO after the crisis was the 2010 IPO of German-based mid-price fashion house Tom Tailor Holding AG. IPOs that were either withdrawn or did not show liquid monthly trading after their public announcement were excluded (criterion (4)).

While many similar studies apply a minimum offer size or offer price, this is not mandatory for inclusion in our data sample. In any case, only two of the sample IPOs considered in this study reported proceeds of less than $1m. After applying all of the above criteria, the final data sample comprises 207 worldwide initial public offerings of fashion and accessories companies with a total IPO volume of roughly $22.1bn in the respective time window.

Table 5.1 shows the geographical distribution of deals with Asia and North America being the two continents with the most active IPO markets. The United States are the single largest market both in terms of number of deals and IPO volumes, followed by Japan and Hong Kong. Europe shows the highest IPO volume due to the two largest deals albeit a rather modest number of transactions. Average IPO underpricing (as measured as the percentage change of the offer price to the closing price one week after the offer) is highest for Chinese IPOs while European and North American deals show lower average underpricing which may be attributed to more established market conditions.

Table 5.1: Fashion IPO geographies, volumes and underpricing[18]

GEOGRAPHICAL AREA	NUMBER OF IPOS	PERCENTAGE	VOLUME (IN $M)	AVERAGE UNDERPRICING
Asia	89	43.00%	5,855.9	24.63%
thereof: China	12	5.80%	1,700.7	55.82%
thereof: Hong Kong	25	12.08%	2,596.4	14.43%
thereof: Japan	28	13.53%	1,031.1	22.30%
Australia	10	4.83%	1,643.7	45.26%
Europe	50	24.15%	8,027.9	11.53%
thereof: Germany	4	1.93%	1,645.7	0.00%
thereof: France	10	4.83%	183.9	13.33%
thereof: Italy	9	4.35%	1,472.6	3.86%
thereof: United Kingdom	7	3.38%	996.9	26.08%
North America	55	26.57%	5,872.2	17.47%
thereof: United States	52	25.12%	5,429.9	16.73%
South America	3	1.45%	702.0	3.36%
TOTAL	**207**	**100.00%**	**22,101.8**	**20.53%**

[18] Underpricing percentages were available on the SDC database for 109 of 207 sample IPOs.

We also observe the seasonality of initial public offerings in the fashion industry. Table 5.2 illustrates the distribution and volumes of IPOs as well as their average underpricing per year. The data show a concentration of deals in time periods such as the end of the 1990s and the years prior to the financial crisis of 2008. This indication supports the hypothesis that companies take advantage of investor sentiment and "hot market" phases when issuing equity.

Table 5.2: Fashion IPO distributions, volumes and underpricing per year

IPO YEAR	NUMBER OF IPOS	PERCENTAGE	VOLUME (IN $M)	PERCENTAGE	AVERAGE UNDERPRICING
1990	1	0.48%	48.1	0.22%	20.18%
1991	3	1.45%	123.8	0.56%	0.00%
1992	9	4.35%	382.1	1.73%	5.16%
1993	13	6.28%	809.7	3.66%	19.78%
1994	20	9.66%	850.1	3.85%	2.20%
1995	11	5.31%	2,585.2	11.70%	1.89%
1996	7	3.38%	443.5	2.01%	16.67%
1997	17	8.21%	1,626.5	7.36%	11.24%
1998	14	6.76%	719.8	3.26%	7.00%
1999	12	5.80%	1,018.0	4.61%	9.66%
2000	15	7.25%	889.4	4.02%	5.47%
2001	6	2.90%	2,159.2	9.77%	-8.52%
2002	7	3.38%	683.8	3.09%	20.27%
2003	12	5.80%	702.7	3.18%	20.30%
2004	14	6.76%	2,399.8	10.86%	26.93%
2005	12	5.80%	886.9	4.01%	33.65%
2006	12	5.80%	1,625.5	7.35%	29.01%
2007	22	10.63%	4,147.7	18.77%	28.18%
TOTAL	**207**	**100.00%**	**22,101.8**	**100.00%**	**20.53%**

Initial underpricing strongly increases in these phases (especially in the years from 2002 to 2007), which further supports the rationale behind the investor sentiment hypothesis for equity issuances. In line with previous empirical research, fashion companies left an average percentage of 20.5% of their offer proceeds on the table. IPO volumes are mainly driven by a few large deals such as those of adidas AG in 1995 and Inditex SA in 2001 and therefore do not show distinctive waves as observed in respect to the number of IPOs conducted.

Finally, we analyze several characteristics of fashion companies conducting an initial public offering. Table 5.3 reports some of the key financials and deal specifics of the sample IPOs. Offer proceeds, the number of shares offered and underpricing have been taken from the SDC/Thomson One Banker Deals database. All company financials have been retrieved from Thomson Financial Datastream and are shown as reported at the end of the IPO year. Firm age at the IPO date was determined using internet research on the respective companies.

Table 5.3: Key financials and IPO characteristics of fashion companies

COMPANY FINANCIALS	MEAN	MEDIAN	MIN	MAX	SKEWNESS	STANDARD DEVIATION
Market capitalization (in $m)	440.58	147.38	0.55	11,883.00	7.64	1,034.29
Sales (in $m)	305.34	135.70	1.70	7,320.80	6.92	666.21
EBIT (in $m)	44.91	18.50	-125.45	809.72	4.75	88.53
Proceeds from offer (in $m)	106.77	36.90	0.48	2,077.56	5.08	237.36
No. of shares offered (in m)	52.18	4.20	0.00	1,988.00	8.96	181.64
Underpricing (in %)	20.53%	12.37%	-32.86%	225.00%	1.63	35.97%
Return on equity (in %)	18.01%	15.92%	-25.61%	81.33%	1.21	16.19%
Firm age at IPO (in years)	28.38	20.00	0.00	156.00	2.10	27.68

The data indicate a concentration of rather small- to medium-sized businesses, although many of the financials are strongly skewed right due to some large outliers. The largest IPO in our data sample is that of Spanish fashion company Inditex SA whose 2001 IPO grossed more than $2.0bn, followed by adidas AG's 1995 $1.5bn offering. Return on equity and EBIT measures indicate that many businesses are solid, profitable companies with strong cash generation which may also be explained with their mature IPO age. With a mean of almost 30 years, the average fashion company is rather advanced in its life cycle when conducting an IPO. The oldest companies in the data sample are French luxury manufacturer Hermès International SA that was founded in 1837 and taken public in 1993 as well as British fashion house Burberry Group plc whose 2002 IPO took place 146 years after its foundation in 1856.

5.3.2 Methodology

Abnormal stock price performance is measured using buy-and-hold returns as suggested by Loughran and Ritter (1995). First, we retrieve monthly stock returns for all fashion IPO companies (R_{jm}) that were adjusted for dividend payments and changes to the capital structure as well as returns on the corresponding local benchmark indices (R_{bm}) from Thomson Financial Datastream. In order to check our results for robustness, we also query monthly returns on corresponding local Datastream equity indices, the Datastream World Market index as well as the Datastream World Clothing & Accessories index.

Barber and Lyon (1997) argue that applying equity indices as a benchmark might bias test results in comparison to the usage of a control-firm approach matched on size and market-to-book ratios. Due to the usage of four different corresponding equity indices, however, we feel that test results are robust and coherent in our analysis. Buy-and-hold returns for sample companies (BHR_{jm}) and corresponding indices (BHR_{bm}) are calculated as follows:

$$(1)\quad BHR_{jm} = \prod_{i=1}^{M}(1 + R_{jm}) \text{ and } BHR_{bm} = \prod_{i=1}^{M}(1 + R_{bm})$$

In a next step, we calculate buy-and-hold abnormal returns (BHAR) for the event windows of 1, 3, 6, 12, 18, 24, 30 and 36 months following the initial public offering by subtracting BHR for the corresponding indices from the BHR for fashion IPO companies:

$$(2)\quad BHAR_{jm} = BHR_{jm} - BHR_{bm}$$

Means and medians for BHAR of all sample IPO companies are tested for statistical significance at conventional levels using a parametric standard t-test statistic, the skewness-adjusted test statistic of Johnson (1978) as well as a non-parametric Wilcoxon signed-rank test for medians. We also apply this approach to a number of univariate sub-samples that differentiate IPOs according to their issue date, issuer SIC code and underwriter reputation.

We further apply cross-sectional regression analysis to identify the key drivers of the long-term stock price performance of fashion IPO companies. The buy-and-hold abnormal returns for the 36-month event window are used as the dependent variable. A series of company- and deal-specific criteria are applied as independent variables. Company financials are taken from the end of the year in which the IPO was conducted. As a measure for the market valuation level at the IPO date, we consider the price/earnings ratio of the corresponding Datastream World Clothing & Accessories index (Erxleben and Schiereck (2010)). Underpricing is defined as the percentage change between the offer price and the closing price one week after public trading began.

"Fashion manufacturer", "secondary shares issue", "foreign IPO", "Asian offering", "underwriter reputation" and "venture capital-backed" are binary dummy variables. "Fashion manufacturer" takes on the value 1 if the issuing company has a two-digit SIC code within the major group "23" and 0 if it carries a "56" SIC code. The variables "secondary shares issue", "foreign IPO", "Asian offering" and "venture capital-backed" are denominated 1 in case the SDC/Thomson One Banker Deals database states that secondary shares were sold in the offering, the issuer is a non-domestic firm, the company was listed on an Asian stock exchange and a venture capital firm took the company public, respectively. "Underwriter reputation" is measured following the approach of Derrien and Kecskés (2007) and takes on the value 1 if the underwriter is a global investment bank. In our specification of global investment banks, we rely on the list presented in Derrien and Kecskés (2007) as well as the global IPO league tables of the SDC/Thomson One Banker Deals database.

We apply four different models in our analysis. While models M1, M2 and M3 include all 207 sample IPOs, model M4 only considers the 109 offerings for which initial underpricing data was available on the SDC/Thomson One Banker Deals database. The heteroscedasticity-consistent test procedure of White (1980) is used to test our results for statistical significance. As a check for robustness, we also apply a standard OLS regression model. Results are tested for autocorrelation using the test statistic of Durbin and Watson (1950, 1951).

Finally, we use the real options framework that has been illustrated for seasoned equity offerings by Carlson et al. (2006, 2010) in the context of our fashion IPO data sample. First, we analyze the development of several issuing company financials and ratios taken from the WorldScope database for one year prior to four years following the IPOs. We further check the SDC/Thomson One Banker Deals database for the denominated use of IPO proceeds. In a last step, we analyze changes in IPO companies' systematic risk exposure. We therefore use an OLS regression of corresponding local equity index returns on the respective monthly IPO returns and a 12-month rolling window for the three post-IPO trading years in order to calculate company betas.

5.4 RESULTS

Table 5.4 shows the results of our buy-and-hold event study for the 207 sample IPOs. While means for BHAR for the first year of trading are positive and medians are negative, but not significant at conventional levels, median buy-and-hold abnormal returns for the following two years are negative and highly significant at the 1% level, peaking at an underperformance of -31.48% for the 36 months following the offering. Due to some positive outliers, means are not statistically significant in most cases of parametrical test procedures, although BHAR of -12.34% for 30 months are still quite considerable. We however find a strong long-term underperformance of fashion IPO companies compared to their respective local market indices based on non-parametric Wilcoxon tests. We also apply three additional equity indices to check our results for robustness. Our findings, however, remain qualitatively the same.

Table 5.4: Long-term event study results for fashion IPO companies

HOLDING PERIOD	BHAR		T-TEST		JOHNSON-TEST		WILCOXON SIGNED-RANK TEST		NOBS
Months	Mean	Median	t-value	p-value	J-value	p-value	z-score	p-value	No.
1	1.60%	-2.94%	1.003	31.72%	1.005	31.62%	-0.479	63.22%	207
3	2.58%	-0.48%	1.194	23.37%	1.197	23.28%	-0.363	71.68%	207
6	6.03%	-4.51%	1.669*	9.66%	1.678*	9.48%	-0.151	88.02%	207
12	1.05%	-12.00%	0.218	82.74%	0.220	82.62%	-1.240	21.49%	207
18	-3.77%	-19.94%	-0.629	53.00%	-0.626	53.21%	-2.786***	0.53%	207
24	-9.84%	-29.93%	-1.475	14.18%	-1.468	14.36%	-3.377***	0.07%	207
30	-12.34%	-30.69%	-1.671*	9.62%	-1.663*	9.79%	-3.516***	0.04%	207
36	-9.45%	-31.48%	-1.114	26.66%	-1.109	26.89%	-3.203***	0.14%	207

***, **, and * indicate statistical significance at the 1%, 5%, and 10% levels, respectively.

We also apply a set of univariate sub-samples to gain first indications of differences in the long-term performance of fashion IPOs. First, we split the data sample into 107 offerings conducted in the 1990s and 100 deals between 2000 and 2007. The data in table 5.5 show that means and medians for IPOs in the latter group are less negative and mostly not significant while offerings conducted in the 1990s show a more significant underperformance.

Positive outliers, however, seem to occur more frequently in the 2000s as is confirmed by the larger difference between mean and median buy-and-hold abnormal returns. Mean BHAR for the first six months of trading have positive values of up to 12% and are statistically significant for 2000s IPOs which confirms the increase in initial underpricing during this period as reported in table 5.2. The differences between mean BHAR for the two sub-samples, however, are only statistically significant for the one-month holding period.

Table 5.5: 1990s and 2000s fashion IPO sub-samples

	1990S IPOs (N=107)				2000S IPOs (N=100)				
Holding Period	BHAR		Johnson-Test	Wilcoxon signed-rank test	BHAR		Johnson-Test	Wilcoxon signed-rank test	Two-sample t-Test
Months	Mean	Median	J-value	z-score	Mean	Median	J-value	z-score	t-value
1	-1.08%	-5.16%	-0.498	-1.632	4.47%	-0.98%	1.912*	-0.980	-1.744*
3	-0.28%	-3.74%	-0.093	-0.945	5.65%	3.94%	1.821*	-1.437	-1.373
6	0.50%	-12.80%	0.110	-1.324	11.95%	6.18%	2.194**	-1.234	-1.589
12	0.07%	-14.58%	0.012	-1.439	2.11%	-11.82%	0.357	-0.268	-0.21
18	-7.55%	-26.50%	-0.801	-3.021***	0.27%	-11.31%	0.039	-0.860	-0.651
24	-19.11%	-40.09%	-1.870*	-3.770***	0.08%	-15.85%	0.011	-0.846	-1.442
30	-18.75%	-36.26%	-1.680*	-3.124***	-5.47%	-27.13%	-0.561	-1.726*	-0.898
36	-21.52%	-37.62%	-1.966*	-3.127***	3.46%	-27.06%	0.269	-1.296	-1.475

***, **, and * indicate significance at 1%, 5%, and 10% levels, respectively.

Table 5.6: Fashion manufacturer and retailer IPO sub-samples

	FASHION MANUFACTURERS (N=129)				FASHION RETAILERS (N=78)				
Holding Period	**BHAR**		**Johnson-Test**	**Wilcoxon signed-rank test**	**BHAR**		**Johnson-Test**	**Wilcoxon signed-rank test**	**Two-sample t-Test**
Months	Mean	Median	J-value	z-score	Mean	Median	J-value	z-score	t-value
1	1.76%	-2.94%	0.880	-0.956	1.34%	-3.53%	0.507	-0.182	0.094
3	2.07%	-2.03%	0.793	-0.196	3.43%	4.32%	0.909	-0.615	-0.393
6	3.01%	-4.62%	0.681	-0.807	11.04%	-2.41%	1.813*	-0.799	-1.220
12	-5.01%	-15.90%	-0.961	-1.879*	11.08%	-8.45%	1.187	-0.296	-1.753*
18	-14.52%	-22.82%	-2.179**	-3.537***	13.99%	-8.10%	1.249	-0.132	-2.181**
24	-23.83%	-35.27%	-3.207***	-4.023***	13.31%	-20.97%	1.074	-0.386	-2.545**
30	-25.27%	-39.20%	-2.796***	-3.962***	9.06%	-23.08%	0.726	-0.635	-2.074**
36	-26.11%	-43.52%	-2.710***	-3.774***	18.10%	-22.74%	1.176	-0.371	-2.489**

***, **, and * indicate significance at 1%, 5%, and 10% levels, respectively.

We further divide our sample into fashion manufacturers, i.e. companies carrying a two-digit SIC code in the “23” group, and firms active in the fashion retail segment, i.e. companies with a “56” SIC code (see table 5.6). Again, we find a strong indication for differences in long-term share performance. BHAR for the 129 IPOs of fashion manufacturers are strongly negative and statistically significant for both means and medians while the 78 fashion retailers did not suffer statistically significant underperformance when going public.

Table 5.7: High and low reputation underwriter IPO sub-samples

	HIGH REPUTATION (N=88)				LOW REPUTATION (N=119)				
Holding Period	**BHAR**		**Johnson-Test**	**Wilcoxon signed-rank test**	**BHAR**		**Johnson-Test**	**Wilcoxon signed-rank test**	**Two-sample t-Test**
Months	Mean	Median	J-value	z-score	Mean	Median	J-value	z-score	t-value
1	3.77%	-2.89%	1.458	-0.179	0.00%	-3.82%	0.000	-0.830	0.416
3	5.66%	0.62%	1.795*	-1.223	0.31%	-0.93%	0.108	-0.666	0.878
6	11.17%	-3.81%	1.993**	-0.974	2.23%	-5.34%	0.482	-1.037	1.224
12	3.92%	-13.84%	0.543	-0.374	-1.06%	-11.46%	-0.161	-1.342	0.709
18	0.36%	-16.09%	0.042	-1.157	-6.83%	-21.54%	-0.844	-2.694***	0.291
24	2.85%	-26.38%	0.270	-1.082	-19.22%	-33.68%	-2.258**	-3.500***	1.137
30	2.22%	-25.95%	0.186	-1.415	-23.10%	-32.69%	-2.529**	-3.447***	1.299
36	6.91%	-24.84%	0.481	-1.290	-21.55%	-38.74%	-2.141**	-3.073***	1.247

***, **, and * indicate significance at 1%, 5%, and 10% levels, respectively.

Finally, we also analyze differences in the long-run stock price performance between companies that have been taken public by a prestigious underwriter (N=88) and those that have not (N=119) according to the methodology of

Derrien and Kecskés (2007). In line with the previous literature on underwriter reputation, table 5.7 shows that firms issuing equity with a high reputation investment bank gain negative, but insignificant long-term returns. On the contrary, mean and median BHAR of low underwriter reputation IPOs are strongly negative and significant at the 1% and 5% levels, respectively.

Table 5.8 shows the results of our cross-sectional regression analysis. In our first model, we find additional evidence for our finding that long-term underperformance of IPO stocks stems mainly from offerings conducted by fashion manufacturers. The corresponding dummy variable is negative and significant at the 5% level throughout models M2 and M3 as well, further confirming the fact that the market valuation for fashion retailers, on average, has been more favorable than for manufacturers over the course of our observation period.

Contrary to our expectations, there is an overall positive correlation between the market valuation level as represented by the price/earnings ratio of the Datastream World Clothing & Accessories index and the long-term BHAR without being significant at conventional levels. This is inconsistent with the hypothesis of eroding stock performance in case companies take advantage of so-called "hot issue markets". While table 5.2 certainly shows that IPO activity does occur in wave patterns, we cannot empirically support a negative correlation between the stock market climate and IPO performance in the fashion industry.

Based on previous studies, we further assumed that offerings conducted by foreign issuing companies might underperform compared to offerings of domestic issuers. The non-significant results for the "foreign IPO" dummy variable in our models contradict this assumption and show that non-domestic offerings have performed rather well. In light of this finding, the case of Prada's and Esprit's Hong Kong IPOs and Tommy Hilfiger's intention for a European offering can be regarded as beneficial strategic decisions and underline the unique characteristics of the fashion industry in international equity financing.

There is no significant correlation between long-run performance and the presence of a venture capital firm or similar financial sponsor. It must be added, however, that VC-backed IPOs only make up 28 deals (13.5%) of our sample. Nevertheless, the "underwriter reputation" dummy has a significantly negative and robust influence on fashion IPO BHAR throughout all models. This is most likely due to the fact that prestigious underwriters (in this case defined as global investment banks) mainly participate in the issuances of larger, more mature companies with lower risk exposures and more stable cash flow generation, but also due to more advanced analyst coverage in the secondary market.

Table 5.8: Results of cross-sectional regression analysis

MODEL	M1	M2	M3	M4
INTERCEPT	**-1.5480****	**-1.4724****	**-1.6127****	-1.4015
	-(2.3260)	-(2.3106)	-(2.3810)	-(1.2288)
DUMMY VARIABLES				
Fashion manufacturer	**-0.3749****	**-0.3713****	**-0.3806****	-0.4246
	-(2.0634)	-(2.0357)	-(2.0845)	-(1.5199)
Secondary shares issue	-0.0832	-0.0716	0.0592	
	-(0.4356)	-(0.3756)	(0.3344)	
Foreign IPO	0.1805	0.1436	0.2546	0.2699
	(0.6133)	(0.4982)	(0.8551)	(0.6634)
Asian offering	0.0895		0.0388	
	(0.5332)		(0.2377)	
Underwriter reputation	**0.4219****	**0.4078***		**0.6534****
	(1.9867)	(1.9696)		(2.4455)
Venture capital-backed	-0.1889	-0.2083	-0.2098	-0.3902
	-(0.9865)	-(1.0870)	-(1.0955)	-(1.5029)
ISSUER FINANCIALS				
Log market cap	0.1100	0.1057	**0.2307***	
	(0.8246)	(0.7905)	(1.6663)	
Return on equity	0.0024	0.0026	0.0026	0.0036
	(0.5052)	(0.5361)	(0.5515)	(0.5485)
Debt ratio	-0.1939	-0.1672	-0.1584	-0.0697
	-(0.5354)	-(0.4659)	-(0.4407)	-(0.1364)
EBIT margin	-0.0918	-0.0970	-0.2871	
	-(0.1645)	-(0.1726)	-(0.5110)	
DEAL CHARACTERISTICS				
Firm age at IPO	**0.16144***	**0.1613***	**0.1694***	**0.2400***
	(1.8882)	(1.8786)	(1.9542)	(1.7368)
Number of bookrunners	0.0133	0.0139	0.0192	
	(0.0820)	(0.0859)	(0.1194)	
Initial underpricing				0.0757
				(0.2023)
CYCLICALITY				
DS World Clothing P/E ratio	0.0335	0.0321	0.0304	0.0264
	(1.6501)	(1.6104)	(1.5240)	(0.5644)
N	207	207	207	109
Adj. R^2	0.0484	0.0519	0.0367	0.0561
F-statistic	**1.8993****	**2.0331****	**1.7001***	**1.7265***
Durbin-Watson test	1.8918	1.8953	1.8863	1.8921

***, ** and * indicate statistical significance at the 1%, 5% and 10% levels, respectively.

When we eliminate the underwriter reputation variable in order to control for the presence of possible multicollinearity in model M3, our central finding is further confirmed by the positive influence of the logarithm of the company's market capitalization at the end of the IPO year that becomes statistically significant. Additionally, the natural logarithm of firm age at the IPO date is significant and positive throughout all four models. Although it might be expected, correlations between firm age, company size as well as the underwriter reputation dummy is not substantial and may therefore be disregarded in our models. It can further be reasoned that IPOs of younger companies significantly underperform those of well-established and mature fashion houses.

According to our analysis, it seems that managerial experience, a long-standing company track record as well as a certain firm size are viewed as critical success factors by equity investors. We therefore conclude that offerings of larger, more mature companies in the fashion and leather accessories industry that are taken public by prestigious underwriting banks significantly outperform IPOs of smaller, inexperienced firms that cannot rely on their heritage or a long period of stable cash flow generation. When we look at the individual buy-and-hold returns of offerings in the fashion and leather accessories industry, many of the companies with strong post-IPO stock price performances are indeed firms that match this very profile such as Abercrombie & Fitch, adidas, Cia Hering, Coach and Hermès International.

In model M4, we only consider the 109 IPOs for which initial underpricing percentages were available on the SDC/Thomson One Banker Deals database. Nevertheless, there is no significant correlation between the amount of money left on the table in the issuance of fashion IPOs and their respective long-term buy-and-hold returns in the three trading years after the offering. Model M4 still supplies further confirmation for our main findings that especially underwriter reputation and firm age at the IPO date positively influence stock returns following an IPO in the fashion and leather accessories industry.

In order to analyze shifts in systematic risk exposure following fashion equity offerings, we further investigate the development of IPO companies' pre- and post-transaction financials that might give an insight in the use of offer proceeds. Table 5.9 shows that the sample companies experience strong growth in both sales and total assets especially in the two years following an IPO. Since capital expenditures also increase after an offering and cash and short-term investments slightly drop in the second year after an IPO, we assume that many companies indeed use their offer proceeds for both investments in internal growth opportunities as well as mergers and acquisitions.

Table 5.9: Company financials in years relative to the IPO date

COMPANY FINANCIALS	YEARS RELATIVE TO THE IPO DATE				
	[-1]	[+1]	[+2]	[+3]	[+4]
Sales (in $m)	294.41	345.16	410.83	470.12	540.81
Sales growth (in %)	*n.a.*	*17.24%*	*19.03%*	*14.43%*	*15.04%*
Total assets (in $m)	210.23	264.37	320.99	362.48	412.42
Total asset growth (in %)	*n.a.*	*25.75%*	*21.42%*	*12.92%*	*13.78%*
Cash & Equivalents (in $m)	21.57	44.42	43.01	55.87	66.65
Cash & Equivalents growth (in %)	*n.a.*	*105.89%*	*-3.16%*	*29.88%*	*19.30%*
Debt ratio (in %)	22.91%	19.74%	19.52%	19.98%	22.31%
Capex / sales (in %)	5.39%	7.08%	5.92%	5.09%	4.65%

This hypothesis is indeed confirmed by data taken from the SDC/Thomson One Banker Deals database which states that 73 out of the 207 issuing sample firms (35.3%) intended to use their offer proceeds for either "future acquisitions", "project finance" or "capital expenditures". In comparison, only 37 sample companies (17.9%) stated that the reduction of their indebtedness or the refinancing of bank loans and other outstanding debt instruments was their primary motivation for raising equity capital in an IPO.

Figure 5.1: Post-IPO mean beta development of fashion companies

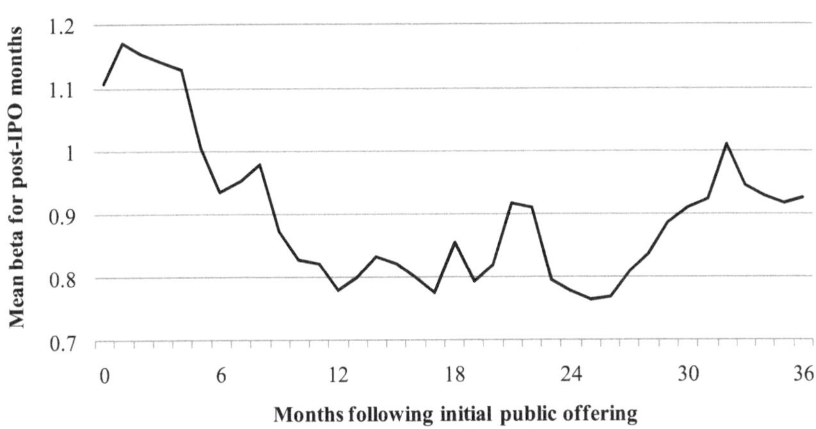

Given the fact that a large fraction of IPO companies use their offer proceeds for investments in internal as well as external growth opportunities, an analysis of changes in systematic risk exposure is made worthwhile. If companies invest in a corporate project such as an M&A transaction, they exercise risky real options in their portfolios and turn them into assets in place that inherently carry lower risk. We therefore hypothesize that IPO companies' betas should significantly decrease following an initial public offering. The data in figure 5.1 clearly confirm these assumptions. The IPO firms' mean beta gradually decreases from a peak of 1.17 two months after the IPO down to 0.77 approximately two years after the offering as also reported by Carlson et al. (2010).

Over the course of our observation period from 1990 to 2007, leading equity indices such as the S&P 500, DAX 30, CAC 40 and FTSE 100 have yielded geometric average returns of 8.0% to 10.0% annually. Given these average returns, a drop in IPO company betas of 0.4 as reported in our analysis would translate into a considerable decrease in demanded equity returns of between 320 and 400 basis points. The strong and statistically significant underperformance of fashion IPO stocks in the three years after conducting their first public equity offering therefore has to be somewhat put into perspective.

While not all issuing companies intended to use their proceeds for the realization of growth opportunities, this can still be upheld for a considerable portion. We have shown empirically that mean betas for our sample companies decrease in the three years after an IPO. In the context of the risk-return spectrum, this reduction of systematic risk exposure helps to explain at least a part of the seemingly poor post-IPO stock price performance. We conclude that the pessimistic outlook on long-term performance in the fashion and leather accessories industry that is given in our buy-and-hold event study should be complemented by the positive effects of systematic risk reduction following IPOs.

5.5 CONCLUSION

We analyze the long-term stock price performance of 207 initial public offerings in the fashion and leather accessories industry between 1990 and 2007. In line with a large fraction of previous research on equity offerings, we find a highly significant underperformance of IPO stocks compared to various corresponding benchmark indices. Univariate sub-samples indicate that this underperformance is mainly driven by IPOs conducted in the 1990s, offerings of fashion manufacturers as opposed to fashion retailers as well as companies that were not taken public by a prestigious, global investment bank. We also find a clustering of IPO activity during phases of high market valuations as well as an average underpricing of 20.5% that strongly increases during hot issue markets.

Cross-sectional regression analysis confirms the underwriter reputation hypothesis and shows that deal execution by a prestigious underwriter significantly improves post-IPO stock price performance. Additionally, company sizes as well as firm age at the IPO date positively affect long-term buy-and-hold returns for fashion companies. We therefore conclude that investors positively evaluate managerial experience and the presence of institutional factors such as global investment banks and a sufficient track record of positive cash flow generation. An empirical correlation between the initial underpricing and the long-term stock price performance cannot be substantiated with our analysis.

We also find a new explanation for the seemingly poor long-term stock price performance when we observe company financials, use of proceeds and changes in post-IPO systematic risk exposure of issuing firms. Many fashion companies use at least parts of their offer proceeds to invest in both internal and external growth opportunities. In doing this, they transform risky real options into lower-risk assets in place. An analysis of changes in fashion IPO companies' mean betas supports this hypothesis and therefore helps to explain that the apparent underperformance of fashion IPO stocks may well be driven by a general reduction in systematic risk. This finding sheds a more optimistic light on initial public offerings as a means to raise capital in the fashion and leather accessories industry. Prada's recent $2.1bn offering has further shown that fashion IPOs are still able to spark investor interest.

6 CONCLUSION AND OUTLOOK

In this dissertation, we investigated four empirical corporate finance-related research questions and gave detailed insights on mergers and acquisitions, divestiture activities and initial public offerings in the fashion and leather accessories industry during the previous two decades. This final chapter summarizes our key findings, gives practical advice on upcoming finance activity in the fashion segment and outlines potential future research objectives.

Chapter 2 illustrates the number, geographical and seasonal distribution as well as deal volumes of 192 M&A transactions in the apparel industry between 1994 and 2009. On average, capital market reactions to deal announcements are distinctively positive as bidding shareholders gain significant cumulative abnormal returns in a short-term event window. When transaction- and acquirer-specific characteristics are accounted for in our cross-sectional regression analysis, M&A transactions of smaller fashion companies with high pre-merger profitability that make only few carefully selected acquisitions earn the highest abnormal returns upon announcement.

On the contrary, deals of larger, multi-brand firms with high takeover frequencies exert a significantly more negative influence on average CAR. The same applies to bull-market transactions as opposed to phases of low market valuations or recessions. It can therefore be further reasoned that equity investors carefully evaluate transaction announcements in their investment decisions. M&A deals conducted by small fashion businesses for the purpose of reducing the high risk exposure that is inherent in the fast-paced apparel industry with its extremely short product life cycles significantly outperform large-scale transactions of brand-collecting conglomerates and multiple bidders.

Chapter 3 advances the previous short-term- and capital market-oriented analysis and further investigates the long-term performance of accounting measures following sample M&A transactions. Due to the non-availability of sufficient balance sheet data, 32 deals have to be eliminated from the analysis, leaving a remaining data sample size of 160 bidder transactions. Accounting measures under consideration include ratios of operating performance, financial leverage as well as sales growth rates of pre- and post-merger years.

Contradictory to the generally positive short-term shareholder wealth effects reported in chapter 2, operating performance of merging companies deteriorates significantly in the three post-merger years in comparison to both pre-merger financials as well as corresponding non-acquiring peer group firms. Results are robust across both size- and performance-matched peer groups as well as three different profitability ratios. On the other hand, measures of financial leverage significantly increase in post-merger years, most likely due to higher debt capacities as a consequence of merger-induced size effects, lower default risk and stronger bargaining power in bank negotiations.

Considering the key drivers of accounting performance, cross-sectional regression analysis shows a distinctively negative correlation between increases in financial leverage and post-merger operating performance. It therefore seems that some of the sample companies have extended their leverage ratios well beyond the optimal degree of corporate indebtedness. Again, the overall stock market valuation climate (as represented by the price/earnings ratio of a corresponding fashion equity index) has a strongly negative effect on merger success. This finding is in line with the drivers of short-term announcement effects in chapter 2 and shows that bull-market transactions generally seem to have a more pessimistic outlook on M&A profitability.

In general, it could be reasoned from our most basic findings of chapters 2 and 3 that fashion M&A transactions are welcomed by equity investors upon their announcement, but are doomed for inferior operating performance in the long run. An investigation of the drivers of merger success as put forward in our cross-sectional regression analyses, however, paints a more refined picture of M&A success factors. Size-enhancing, all-cash financed "empire-building" transactions of multiple bidders significantly underperform selective and well-considered strategic deals conducted in times of sparse cash resources in terms of both short-term shareholder wealth effects as well as long-term operating performance. This gives a more sophisticated and insightful outlook on future mergers and acquisitions in the fashion and accessories industry.

While there has been large-scale and frequent M&A activity, divestitures in the apparel segment are rather scarce and of lower magnitude in terms of deal volumes. Nevertheless, this does not necessarily mean that fashion companies could not benefit from the disposal of a subsidiary or portfolio brand. In chapter 4, we illustrate the particularly prominent German case of once-highly successful ladies wear manufacturer ESCADA AG that finally went bankrupt following a series of strategic deficits and poor governance in August 2009.

Despite numerous announcements of intended disposal plans, the company adhered to its largest non-core segment PRIMERA AG with whom it barely shared any synergies for almost an entire decade. Estimated proceedings from a potential divestiture of up to €200m would have endowed ESCADA with sufficient liquidity for the implementation of much-needed restructuring measures and for the purpose of debt refinancing. Management, however, apparently suffered from a strong case of loss aversion, status quo bias and escalating commitment in its decision-making process to sell off the subsidiary. While a disposal of the non-core segment alone might not have saved ESCADA from its ultimate bankruptcy, it would have definitely been an important measure as part of a successful and holistic turnaround program.

Chapter 5 reviews IPO activity, initial returns, long-term stock price performance and changes in systematic risk exposure following 207 initial public offerings in the fashion industry. Although issuing companies gain average initial returns of 20.5%, they significantly underperform corresponding equity indices over the course of a three year post-IPO buy-and-hold period. In line with previous research, this underperformance is mainly driven by small growth companies that have not been taken public by a prestigious underwriter.

There is also a more general finding on the causes of the seemingly poor stock price performance of fashion IPO companies. A large fraction of issuing firms intended to use their offer proceeds for future acquisitions and similar growth opportunities. Company financials indeed show that capital expenditures and total asset volumes increase in post-IPO years, underlining the assumption that the sample firms exercise existing real options in their company portfolios. An analysis of company betas confirms the hypothesis that systematic risk exposure should therefore decrease after an offering. We conclude that long-term buy-and-hold returns do indeed not only reflect poor performance, but rather a general reduction of post-IPO company risk.

In summary, we have given a variety of empirical insights into a highly dynamic business segment that has been widely disregarded in previous empirical finance research. The ongoing consolidation activity in the fashion and accessories industry appears in a mixed light considering the large differences between positive announcement effects and eroding post-merger operating performance in our analyses. Looking at the key drivers of M&A success however reveals that carefully evaluated, strategic deals consistently outperform random "hot market" acquisitions in both capital market- and accounting-oriented merger perspectives. The availability of attractive potential takeover targets in the apparel industry as well as the fashion conglomerates' enduring pursuit of their brand-collecting strategies in recent years suggest that M&A activity will continue to be an integral component of industry development in the future.

Using the example of ESCADA AG's insolvency, we have illustrated the fast-changing dynamics and high risk exposure that even considerably large and established companies in the fashion industry face. While the refocusing on ESCADA's core competencies in the luxury apparel business would have been a beneficial corporate decision, further operating turnaround measures would have had to be implemented for the company to return to its former profitability and customer appreciation. In our opinion, strategic reorientation as well as situations of financial distress will linger on as the two main drivers behind divestiture activities while the rest of the fashion industry is rather concentrating on internal and external growth strategies.

Finally, our analysis of buy-and-hold returns following initial public offerings in the fashion and accessories industry shows a significant underperformance of newly-issued stocks compared to benchmark indices. While this finding is basically in line with most previous research on long-term offer performance, we put this generally negative outlook into perspective using a beta analysis that shows a strong reduction in systematic risk exposure of issuing firms. If fashion companies continue to use their proceeds from an initial public offering for the realization of growth options, this pattern can be assumed to uphold for future offerings as well. Rumors about upcoming IPOs of well-known fashion houses such as Salvatore Ferragamo and Versace indicate that equity issuances will be an attractive financing option for the time to come.

Still, there are some further research objectives that we did not explicitly address in this dissertation and that leave room for future studies on financing activity in the fashion industry. First of all, a more detailed differentiation between manufacturing companies and retailers might reveal additional insights into two different business models. Furthermore, we concentrated on rather large observation windows of between 15 and 20 years while it might also be of interest for future research to divide these sample periods into shorter time horizons to illustrate dynamic developments of M&A announcement effects, changes in operating performance and IPO activity over time. Lastly, there is also a lack of clinical papers on the merger strategies and M&A success perspectives of particular companies such as the huge brand-collecting fashion conglomerates in order to give a more tangible outlook on target screening, strategic M&A decisions and post-merger integration efforts.

On a more general level, we hope that this dissertation will encourage further industry-specific research studies. While we have focused on the fashion and accessories segment, many other industries exhibit idiosyncratic characteristics and drivers of business that make independent analyses worthwhile. Many factors such as product and industry life cycles, changes in customer behavior and shifts in supply and demand structures distinguish certain industries from others. Therefore, corporate finance activity in particular will always mirror these idiosyncrasies and show distinctive patterns across various industries.

BIBLIOGRAPHY

Abernathy, F. H., Dunlop, J. T., Hammond, J. H., Weil, D., Bresnahan, T. F., & Pashigian, B. P. (1995). The Information-Integrated Channel: A Study of The U.S. Apparel Industry in Transition. *Brookings Papers on Economic Activity. Microeconomics, 1995* (1), 175-246.

Aggarwal, R., & Kyaw, N. A. (2010). Capital Structure, Dividend Policy, and Multinationality: Theory versus Empirical Evidence. *International Review of Financial Analysis, 19* (2), 140-150.

Agrawal, A., Jaffe, J. F., & Mandelker, G. N. (1992). The Post Merger Performance of Acquiring Firms. *The Journal of Finance, 47* (4), 1605-1621.

Ahnefeld, M., Keisers, M., & Schiereck, D. (2006). Wertgenerierung durch M&A-Transaktionen in der internationalen Wasserwirtschaft. *Die Unternehmung, 60* (6), 427-442.

Allais, M. (1953). Le Comportement de l'Homme Rationnel devant le Risque: Critique des Postulats et Axiomes de l'Ecole Americaine. *Econometrica, 21* (4), 503-546.

Andrade, G., Mitchell, M., & Stafford, E. (2001). New Evidence and Perspectives on Mergers. *The Journal of Economic Perspectives, 15* (2), 103-120.

Ang, J. S., & Boyer, C. (2009). Has the 1987 Crash Changed the Psyche of the Stock Market? The Evidence from Initial Public Offerings. *Review of Accounting and Finance, 8* (2), 138-154.

Angelidis, T., & Andrikopoulos, A. (2010). Idiosyncratic Risk, Returns and Liquidity in the London Stock Exchange: A Spillover Approach. *International Review of Financial Analysis, 19* (3), 214-221.

Asquith, P., Bruner, R., & Mullins, D. (1983). The Gains to Bidding Firms from Merger. *Journal of Financial Economics, 11* (1-4), 121-133.

Baker, M., & Wurgler, J. (2007). Investor Sentiment in the Stock Market. *The Journal of Economic Perspectives, 21* (2), 129-151.

Barber, B. M., & Lyon, J. D. (1996). Detecting Abnormal Operating Performance: The Empirical Power and Specification of Test Statistics. *Journal of Financial Economics, 41* (3), 359-399.

Barber, B. M., & Lyon, J. D. (1997). Detecting Long-Run Abnormal Stock Returns: The Empirical Power and Specification of Test Statistics. *Journal of Financial Economics, 43* (3), 341-372.

Barberis, N., & Huang, M. (2001). Mental Accounting, Loss Aversion, and Individual Stock Returns. *The Journal of Finance, 56* (4), 1247-1292.

Barberis, N., Huang, M., & Santos, T. (2001). Prospect Theory and Asset Prices. *The Quarterly Journal of Economics, 116* (1), 1-53.

Barberis, N., Huang, M., & Thaler, R. H. (2006). Individual Preferences, Monetary Gambles, and Stock Market Participation: A Case for Narrow Framing. *The American Economic Review, 96* (4), 1069-1090.

Barry, C. B., Muscarella, C. J., Peavy, J. W., & Vetsuypens, M. R. (1990). The Role of Venture Capital in the Creation of Public Companies. *Journal of Financial Economics, 27* (2), 447-471.

Bassen, A., Schiereck, D., & Wübben, B. (2010). M&A Success of German Acquisitions in the US - Evidence from Capital Market and Survey Data. *Applied Financial Economics, 20* (7), 543-559.

Beatty, R. P., & Ritter, J. R. (1986). Investment Banking, Reputation, and the Underpricing of Initial Public Offerings. *Journal of Financial Economics, 15* (1-2), 213-232.

Becker, G. S. (1962). Irrational Behavior and Economic Theory. *The Journal of Political Economy, 70* (1), 1-13.

Beitel, P., Schiereck, D., & Wahrenburg, M. (2004). Explaining M&A Success in European Banks. *European Financial Management, 10* (1), 109-139.

Benartzi, S., & Thaler, R. H. (1995). Myopic Loss Aversion and the Equity Premium Puzzle. *The Quarterly Journal of Economics, 110* (1), 73-92.

Benveniste, L. M., & Spindt, P. A. (1989). How Investment Bankers Determine the Offer Price and Allocation of New Issues. *Journal of Financial Economics, 24* (2), 343-361.

Berry, K. (2000). Excess Returns in Electric Utility Mergers during Transition to Competition. *Journal of Regulatory Economics, 18* (2), 175-188.

Bessler, W., & Kurth, A. (2007). Agency Problems and the Performance of Venture-Backed IPOs in Germany: Exit Strategies, Lock-Up Periods, and Bank Ownership. *The European Journal of Finance, 13* (1), 29-63.

Betzer, A., & Goergen, M. (2009). *Disentangling the Link between Stock and Accounting Performance in Acquisitions*. Working paper, European Corporate Governance Institute.

Bhattacharyya, S., & Nain, A. S. (2011). Horizontal Acquisitions and Buying Power: A Product Market Analysis. *Journal of Financial Economics, 99* (1), 97-115.

Bikhchandani, S., Hirshleifer, D., & Welch, I. (1998). Learning from the Behavior of Others: Conformity, Fads, and Informational Cascades. *The Journal of Economic Perspectives, 12* (3), 151-170.

Binder, J. (1998). The Event Study Methodolody since 1969. *Review of Quantitative Finance and Accounting, 11* (2), 111-137.

Boehmer, E., & Löffler, Y. (1999). Kursrelevante Ereignisse bei Unterneh-mensübernahmen: Eine empirische Analyse des deutschen Kapitalmarkts. *zfbf, 51* (4), 299-324.

Boehmer, E., Musumeci, J., & Poulsen, A. B. (1991). Event-Study Methodology under Conditions of Event-Induced Variance. *Journal of Financial Economics, 30* (2), 253-272.

Bouwman, C. H. S., Fuller, K., & Nain, A. S. (2009). Market Valuation and Acquisition Quality: Empirical Evidence. *The Review of Financial Studies, 22* (2), 633-678.

Brav, A., Geczy, C., & Gompers, P. A. (2000). Is the Abnormal Return Following Equity Issuances Anomalous? *Journal of Financial Economics, 56* (2), 209-249.

Brav, A., & Gompers, P. A. (1997). Myth or Reality? The Long-Run Underperformance of Initial Public Offerings: Evidence from Venture and Nonventure Capital-Backed Companies. *The Journal of Finance, 52* (5), 1791-1821.

Brockner, J. (1992). The Escalation of Commitment to a Failing Course of Action: Toward Theoretical Progress. *Academy of Management Review, 17* (1), 39-61.

Brown, S., & Warner, J. B. (1980). Measuring Security Price Performance. *Journal of Financial Economics, 8* (3), 205-258.

Brown, S., & Warner, J. B. (1985). Using Daily Stock Returns - The Case of Event Studies. *Journal of Financial Economics, 14* (1), 3-31.

Bruner, R. F. (2002). Does M&A Pay? A Survey of Evidence for the Decision-Maker. *Journal of Applied Finance, 12* (1), 48-68.

Campa, J. M., & Hernando, I. (2004). Shareholder Value Creation in European M&As. *European Financial Management, 10* (1), 47-81.

Carlson, M., Fisher, A., & Giammarino, R. (2004). Corporate Investment and Asset Price Dynamics: Implications for the Cross-Section of Returns. *The Journal of Finance, 59* (6), 2577-2603.

Carlson, M., Fisher, A., & Giammarino, R. (2006). Corporate Investment and Asset Price Dynamics: Implications for SEO Event Studies and Long-Run Performance. *The Journal of Finance, 61* (3), 1009-1034.

Carlson, M., Fisher, A., & Giammarino, R. (2010). SEO Risk Dynamics. *The Review of Financial Studies, 23* (11), 4026-4077.

Carmon, Z., & Ariely, D. (2000). Focusing on the Foregone: How Value Can Appear So Different to Buyers and Sellers. *Journal of Consumer Research, 27* (3), 360-370.

Carter, R., Dark, F. H., & Singh, A. K. (1998). Underwriter Reputation, Initial Returns, and the Long-Run Performance of IPO Stocks. *The Journal of Finance, 53* (1), 285-311.

Chang, S.-C., Chung, T.-Y., & Lin, W.-C. (2010). Underwriter Reputation, Earnings Management and the Long-Run Performance of Initial Public Offerings. *Accounting & Finance, 50* (1), 53-78.

Chang, X., Lin, S. H., Tam, L. H. K., & Wong, G. (2010). Cross-Sectional Determinants of Post-IPO Stock Performance: Evidence from China. *Accounting & Finance, 50* (3), 581-603.

Chemmanur, T. J., & Fulghieri, P. (1999). A Theory of the Going-Public Decision. *The Review of Financial Studies, 12* (2), 249-279.

Clement, M., Fischer, M., & Goerke, B. (2007). Neuprodukteinführungen in der Filmindustrie: Wie reagieren Kapitalmarktinvestoren auf den Umsatzerfolg neuer Kinofilme? *Die Betriebswirtschaft, 67* (4), 418-444.

Cooney, J. W., Singh, A. K., Carter, R., & Dark, F. H. (2001). *IPO Initial Returns and Underwriter Reputation: Has the Inverse Relation Flipped in the 1990s?* Working paper, University of Kentucky.

Cooper, I., & Priestley, R. (2011). Real Investment and Risk Dynamics. *Journal of Financial Economics, 101* (1), 182-205.

Cornett, M. M., McNutt, J. J., & Tehranian, H. (2006). Performance Changes Around Bank Mergers: Revenue Enhancements versus Cost Reductions. *Journal of Money, Credit, and Banking, 38* (4), 1013-1050.

Corrado, C. J. (2011). Event Studies: A Methodology Review. *Accounting & Finance, 51* (1), 207-234.

Croci, E., Petmezas, D., & Vagenas-Nanos, E. (2010). Managerial Overconfidence in High and Low Valuation Markets and Gains to Acquisitions. *International Review of Financial Analysis, 19* (5), 368-378.

DeAngelo, H., DeAngelo, L., & Wruck, K. H. (2002). Asset Liquidity, Debt Covenants, and Managerial Discretion in Financial Distress: The Collapse of L.A. Gear. *Journal of Financial Economics, 64* (1), 3-34.

DeLong, G. L. (2001). Stockholder Gains From Focusing versus Diversifying Bank Mergers. *Journal of Financial Economics, 59* (2), 221-252.

DeLong, G. L. (2003). Does Long-Term Performance of Mergers Match Market Expectations? Evidence from the US Banking Industry. *Financial Management, 32* (2), 5-25.

Derrien, F., & Kecskés, A. (2007). The Initial Public Offerings of Listed Firms. *The Journal of Finance, 62* (1), 447-479.

Dhiensiri, N., & Sayrak, A. (2010). The Value Impact of Analyst Coverage. *Review of Accounting and Finance, 9* (3), 306-331.

Dickerson, A., Gibson, H., & Tsakalotos, E. (1997). The Impact of Acquisitions on Company Performance: Evidence from a large Panel of UK Firms. *Oxford Economic Papers, 49* (3), 344-361.

Dolvin, S. D., & Pyles, M. K. (2007). Seasonal Affective Disorder and the Pricing of IPOs. *Review of Accounting and Finance, 6* (2), 214-228.

Drees, F., Mietzner, M., & Schiereck, D. (2011). *Equity Ownership, Agency Problems and Shareholder Wealth: Understanding the Unique Role of*

Corporate Block Owners. Working paper, Darmstadt University of Technology and Zeppelin University.

Durbin, J., & Watson, G. S. (1950). Testing for Serial Correlation in Least Squares Regression. I. *Biometrika, 37* (3-4), 409-428.

Durbin, J., & Watson, G. S. (1951). Testing for Serial Correlation in Least Squares Regression. I. *Biometrika, 38* (1-2), 159-177.

Eckbo, B. E., Masulis, R. W., & Norli, O. (2007). Security Offerings. In B. E. Eckbo (Ed.), *Handbook of Corporate Finance* (Vol. 1). Amsterdam: Elsevier B.V.

Eckbo, B. E., & Norli, O. (2005). Liquidity Risk, Leverage, and Long-Run IPO Returns. *Journal of Corporate Finance, 11* (1-2), 1-35.

Eckbo, B. E., & Thorburn, K. S. (2000). Gains to Bidder Firms Revisited: Domestic and Foreign Acquisitions in Canada. *Journal of Financial and Quantitative Analysis, 35* (1), 1-25.

Erxleben, U., & Schiereck, D. (2010). *Wealth Creation of Mergers in Downturn Markets: Evidence from European M&A*. Working paper, Darmstadt University of Technology.

Fama, E. F. (1970). Efficient Capital Markets: A Review of Theory and Empirical Work. *The Journal of Finance, 25* (2), 383-417.

Fama, E. F., Fisher, L., Jensen, M. C., & Roll, R. (1969). The Adjustment of Stock Prices to New Information. *International Economic Review, 10* (1), 1-21.

Firth, M. (1980). Takeovers, Shareholder Returns, and the Theory of the Firm. *The Quarterly Journal of Economics, 94* (2), 235-260.

Fischer, C. (2000). *Why Do Firms Go Public? Empirical Evidence from Germany's Neuer Markt.* Working paper, Ludwig-Maximilians-Universität München.

Francis, R. N. (2010). The Relative Information Content of Operating and Financing Cash Flow in the Proposed Cash Flow Statement. *Accounting & Finance, 50* (4), 829-851.

Franks, J., Harris, R., & Titman, S. (1991). The Postmerger Share-price Performance of Acquiring Firms. *Journal of Financial Economics, 29* (1), 81-96.

Fridolfsson, S.-O., & Stennek, J. (2005). Why Mergers Reduce Profits and Raise Share Prices - A Theory of Preemptive Mergers. *Journal of the European Economic Association, 3* (5), 1083-1104.

Fuller, K., Netter, J., & Stegemoller, M. (2002). What do Returns to Acquiring Firms Tell us? Evidence from Firms that make many Acquisitions. *The Journal of Finance, 57* (4), 1763-1793.

Gertner, R. H., & Stillman, R. S. (2001). Vertical Integration and Internet Strategies in the Apparel Industry. *The Journal of Industrial Economics, 49* (4), 417-440.

Gervais, S., Heaton, J. B., & Odean, T. (2001). Learning To Be Overconfident. *Review of Financial Studies, 14* (1), 1-27.

Ghosh, A. (2001). Does Operating Performance Really Improve following Corporate Acquisitions? *Journal of Corporate Finance, 7* (2), 151-178.

Ghosh, A., & Jain, P. J. (2000). Financial Leverage Changes Associated with Corporate Mergers. *Journal of Corporate Finance, 6* (4), 377-402.

Glasmeier, A., Thompson, J. W., & Kays, A. J. (1993). The Geography of Trade Policy: Trade Regimes and Location Decisions in the Textile and Apparel Complex. *Transactions of the Institute of British Geographers, 18* (1), 19-35.

Goergen, M., & Renneboog, L. (2004). Shareholder Wealth Effects of European Domestic and Cross-border Takeover Bids. *European Financial Management, 10* (1), 9-45.

Hagendorff, J., & Keasey, K. (2009). Post-merger Strategy and Performance: Evidence from the US and European Banking Industries. *Accounting & Finance, 49* (4), 725-751.

Haigh, M. S., & List, J. A. (2006). Do Professional Traders Exhibit Myopic Loss Aversion? An Experimental Analysis. *The Journal of Finance, 60* (1), 523-534.

Hanemann, W. M. (1991). Willingness to Pay and Willingness to Accept: How Much Can They Differ? *The American Economic Review, 81* (3), 635-647.

Harrington, S. E., & Shrider, D. G. (2007). All Events Induce Variance: Analyzing Abnormal Returns When Effects Vary across Firms. *Journal of Financial and Quantitative Analysis, 42* (1), 229-256.

Hartmann, I., Bassen, A., & Schiereck, D. (2007). Langfristige Kursentwicklung und operativer Erfolg von ausländischen Emittenten in Deutschland. *Bankarchiv, 55* (5), 368-399.

Healy, P., Palepu, K., & Ruback, R. S. (1992). Does Corporate Performance Improve After Mergers? *Journal of Financial Economics, 31* (2), 135-175.

Heaton, J. B. (2002). Managerial Optimism and Corporate Finance. *Financial Management, 31* (2), 33-45.

Houston, J., James, C., & Ryngaert, M. (2001). Where Do Merger Gains Come From? Bank Mergers from the Perspective of Insiders and Outsiders. *Journal of Financial Economics, 60* (2-3), 285-331.

Ibbotson, R. G. (1975). Price Performance of Common Stock New Issues. *Journal of Financial Economics, 2* (3), 235-272.

Jain, B. A., & Martin, C. L. (2005). The Association Between Audit Quality and Post-IPO Performance: A Survival Analysis Approach. *Review of Accounting and Finance, 4* (4), 51-75.

Jarrell, G. A., & Poulsen, A. B. (1989). The Returns to Acquiring Firms in Tender Offers: Evidence from Three Decades. *Financial Management, 18* (3), 12-19.

Jensen, M. C. (1986). Agency Costs of Free Cash Flows, Corporate Finance and Takeovers. *The American Economic Review, 76* (2), 323-329.

Johnson, N. J. (1978). Modified t Tests and Confidence Intervals for Asymmetrical Populations. *Journal of the American Statistical Association, 73* (363), 536-544.

Kahle, K. M., & Walkling, R. A. (1996). The Impact of Industry Classifications on Financial Research. *Journal of Financial and Quantitative Analysis, 31* (3), 309-335.

Kahneman, D., Knetsch, J. L., & Thaler, R. H. (1991). The Endowment Effect, Loss Aversion, and Status Quo Bias. *The Journal of Economic Perspectives, 5* (1), 193-206.

Kahneman, D., & Tversky, A. (1979). Prospect Theory: An Analysis of Decision under Risk. *Econometrica, 47* (2), 263-291.

Kaplan, S. N., & Weisbach, M. S. (1992). The Success of Acquisitions: Evidence from Divestitures. *The Journal of Finance, 47* (1), 107-138.

Kim, Y. S., & Mathur, I. (2008). The Impact of Geographic Diversification on Firm Performance. *International Review of Financial Analysis, 17* (4), 747-766.

Königs, A., & Schiereck, D. (2008). Combined in Luxury - M&A Announcement Effects and Capital Market Integration in Europe. *ICFAI Journal of Mergers & Acquisitions, 5* (1), 30-56.

Kothari, S. P., & Warner, J. B. (2007). Econometrics of Event Studies. In B. E. Eckbo (Ed.), *Handbook of Corporate Finance* (Vol. 1). Amsterdam: Elsevier B.V.

KPMG. (2009). Herausforderungen im deutschen Luxusmarkt - Ergebnisse einer bevölkerungsrepräsentativen Grundlagenstudie (pp. 28). Germany: KPMG AG Wirtschaftsprüfungsgesellschaft.

La Rocca, M., La Rocca, T., Gerace, D., & Smark, C. (2009). Effect of Diversification on Capital Structure. *Accounting & Finance, 49* (4), 799-826.

Laabs, J.-P., & Schiereck, D. (2010). The Long-Term Success of in the Automotive Supply Industry: Determinants of Capital Market Performance. *Journal of Economics and Finance, 34* (1), 61-88.

Langestieg, T. (1978). An Application of a Three-Factor Performance Index to Measure Stockholder Gains from Merger. *Journal of Financial Economics, 6* (4), 365-384.

Lantto, A.-M., & Sahlström, P. (2009). Impact of International Financial Reporting Standard Adoption on Key Financial Ratios. *Accounting & Finance, 49* (2), 341-361.

Loughran, T., & Ritter, J. R. (1995). The New Issues Puzzle. *The Journal of Finance, 50* (1), 23-51.

Loughran, T., & Ritter, J. R. (2002). Why Don't Issuers Get Upset About Leaving Money on the Table in IPOs? *The Review of Financial Studies, 15* (2), 413-443.

Loughran, T., & Ritter, J. R. (2004). Why Has IPO Underpricing Changed Over Time? *Financial Management, 33* (3), 5-37.

Lowry, M., & Shu, S. (2002). Litigation Risk and IPO Underpricing. *Journal of Financial Economics, 65* (3), 309-335.

MacKinlay, A. C. (1997). Event Studies in Economics and Finance. *Journal of Economic Literature, 35* (1), 13-39.

Malestata, P. H. (1983). The Wealth Effect of Merger Activity and the Objective Functions of Merging Firms. *Journal of Financial Economics, 11* (1-4), 155-181.

McWilliams, A., & Siegel, D. (1997). Event Studies in Management Research: Theoretical and Empirical Issues. *Academy of Management Journal, 40* (3), 626-657.

Megginson, W. L., & Weiss, K. A. (1991). Venture Capitalist Certification in Initial Public Offerings. *The Journal of Finance, 46* (3), 879-903.

Mentz, M., & Schiereck, D. (2008). Cross-border Mergers and the Cross-Border Effect: The Case of the Automotive Supply Industry. *Review of Managerial Science, 2* (3), 199-218.

Mitchell, M., & Mulherin, J. H. (1996). The Impact of Industry Shocks on Takeover and Restructuring Activity. *Journal of Financial Economics, 41* (2), 193-229.

Moeller, S. B., Schlingemann, F. P., & Stulz, R. M. (2005). Wealth Destruction on a Massive Scale? A Study of Acquiring-Firm Returns in the Recent Merger Wave. *The Journal of Finance, 60* (2), 757-782.

Mulherin, J. H., & Boone, A. L. (2000). Comparing Acquisitions and Divestitures. *Journal of Corporate Finance, 6* (2), 117-139.

Olibe, K. O., Michello, F. A., & Thorne, J. (2008). Systematic Risk and International Diversification: An Empirical Perspective. *International Review of Financial Analysis, 17* (4), 681-698.

Pagano, M., Panetta, F., & Zingales, L. (1998). Why Do Companies Go Public? An Empirical Analysis. *The Journal of Finance, 53* (1), 27-64.

Poulsen, T. (2011). Private Benefits in Corporate Control Transactions. *International Review of Financial Analysis, 20* (1), 52-58.

Rabin, M., & Thaler, R. H. (2001). Anomalies: Risk Aversion. *The Journal of Economic Perspectives, 15* (1), 219-232.

Ramaswamy, K., & Waegelein, J. (2003). Firm Financial Performance following Mergers. *Review of Quantitative Finance and Accounting, 20* (2), 115-126.

Ravenscraft, D., & Scherer, F. (1989). *Mergers, Sell-Offs, and Economic Efficiency*. Washington D.C.: The Brookings Institution.

Ritter, J. R. (1991). The Long-Run Performance of Initial Public Offering. *The Journal of Finance, 46* (1), 3-27.

Ritter, J. R. (2003). Differences Between European and American IPO Markets. *European Financial Management, 9* (4), 421-434.

Rock, K. (1986). Why New Issues Are Underpriced. *Journal of Financial Economics, 15* (1-2), 187-212.

Roll, R. (1986). The Hubris Hypothesis of Corporate Takeovers. *Journal of Business, 59* (2), 197-216.

Samuelson, W., & Zeckhauser, R. (1988). Status Quo Bias in Decision Making. *Journal of Risk and Uncertainty, 1* (1), 7-59.

Scharfstein, D. S., & Stein, J. C. (1990). Herd Behavior and Investment. *The American Economic Review, 80* (3), 465-479.

Serra, A. P. (2002). *Event Study Tests - A Brief Survey*. Working paper, Universidade do Porto.

Shefrin, H. (1999). *Beyond Greed and Fear: Understanding Behavioral Finance and the Psychology of Investing*. Boston: Oxford University Press.

Shefrin, H. (2001). Behavioral Corporate Finance. *Journal of Applied Corporate Finance, 14* (3), 8-19.

Shefrin, H., & Statman, M. (1985). The Disposition to Sell Winners Too Early and Ride Losers Too Long: Theory and Evidence. *The Journal of Finance, 40* (3), 777-790.

Shiller, R. J. (2000). *Irrational Exuberance*. Princeton: Princeton University Press.

Shogren, J. F., Shin, S. Y., Hayes, D. J., & Kliebenstein, J. B. (1994). Resolving Differences in Willingness to Pay and Willingness to Accept. *The American Economic Review, 84* (1), 255-270.

Shourun, G., Hotchkiss, E. S., & Song, W. (2011). Do Buyouts (Still) Create Value? *The Journal of Finance, 66* (2), 479-517.

Statman, M., & Sepe, J. F. (1989). Project Termination Announcements and the Market Value of the Firm. *Financial Management, 18* (4), 74-81.

Statman, M., & Tyebjee, T. T. (1985). Optimistic Capital Budgeting Forecasts: An Experiment. *Financial Management, 14* (3), 27-33.

Staw, B. M. (1976). Knee-Deep in the Big Muddy: A Study of Escalating Commitment to a Chosen Course of Action. *Organizational Behavior and Human Performance, 16* (1), 27-44.

Suzuki, A. (2009). Market Foreclosure and Vertical Merger: A Case Study of the Vertical Merger Between Turner Broadcasting and Time Warner. *International Journal of Industrial Organization, 27* (4), 532-543.

Thaler, R. H. (1980). Toward a Positive Theory of Consumer Choice. *Journal of Economic Behavior and Organization, 1* (1), 39-60.

Thaler, R. H., Tversky, A., Kahneman, D., & Schwartz, A. (1997). The Effect of Myopia and Loss Aversion on Risk Taking: An Experimental Test. *The Quarterly Journal of Economics, 112* (2), 647-661.

Wansley, J. W., Lane, W. R., & Yang, H. C. (1983). Shareholder Returns to USA Acquired Firms and Domestic Acquisitions. *Journal of Business Finance & Accounting, 10* (4), 647-656.

Welch, I. (1989). Seasoned Offerings, Imitation Costs, and the Underpricing of Initial Public Offerings. *The Journal of Finance, 44* (2), 421-449.

White, H. (1980). A Heteroskedasticity-Consistent Covariance Matrix Estimator and a Direct Test for Heteroskedasticity. *Econometrica, 48* (4), 817-838.

WTO. (2010). *International Trade Statistics 2010.*

Corporate Finance and Governance

Herausgegeben von Dirk Schiereck

Band 1 Sebastian Michael Gläsner: Return Patterns of German Open-End Real Estate Funds. An Empirical Explanation of Smooth Fund Returns. 2010.

Band 2 Patrick Ams: Directors' Dealings and Insider Trading in Germany. An Empirical Analysis. 2010.

Band 3 Joachim Vogt: Value Creation within the Construction Industry. A Study of Strategic Takeovers. 2011.

Band 4 Fabian Braemisch: Underpricing, Long-Run Performance, and Valuation of Initial Public Offerings. 2011.

Band 5 Matthäus Markus Sielecki: Creating and Governing an Integrated Market for Retail Banking Services in Europe. A Conceptual-Empirical Study of the Role of Regulation in Promoting a Single Euro Payments Area. 2011.

Band 6 Arne Wilkes: Determinants of Credit Spreads. An Empirical Analysis for the European Corporate Bond Market. 2011.

Band 7 Dirk Schiereck / Martin Setzer (Hrsg.): Bankerfolg und Akquisitionen. Aktuelle Erkenntnisse zur Konsolidierung und Restrukturierung der Finanzindustrie. 2011.

Band 8 Steffen Meinshausen: M&A Activity, Divestitures and Initial Public Offerings in the Fashion Industry. 2012.

www.peterlang.de

Björn B. Schmidt

The Dynamics of M&A Strategy

Mastering the Outbound M&A Wave of Chinese Banks

Frankfurt am Main, Berlin, Bern, Bruxelles, New York, Oxford, Wien, 2010.
XX, 337 pp., num. tab. and graph.
European University Studies. Series 5: Economics and Management.
Vol. 3366
ISBN 978-3-631-60093-1 · pb. € 65,80*

China's banking sector has witnessed significant inbound M&A traffic by developed market banks in recent years. At the same time, Chinese banks have risen to become some of the world's biggest banks. Along with these massive market values and financing capabilities have come global ambitions culminating in first outbound M&A moves. This study exploratively researches the relationship between developed market banks' inbound M&A into China and Chinese banks' outbound M&A. Based on a conceptual discussion, case studies and expert interviews an explanation model is developed outlining the drivers and barriers of Chinese banks' outbound M&A and the factors in the inbound-outbound relationship. This model enables developed market banks to analyse potential M&A reactions by incumbents. Finally, dynamic M&A market entry strategies are derived, which explicitly account for future incumbent outbound M&A moves.

Content: Market entry in strategic management · Static versus dynamic analysis · The action-response dyad and firm interaction · Research status · The explanatory value of the market-based view and of supplementing theoretical approaches · Case studies of Chinese outbound M&A · Semi-structured expert interviews · Dynamic M&A market entry explanation model · Recommended courses of action · Examples of dynamic M&A market entry strategies · Research and management contribution and implications

FSC
www.fsc.org
MIX
Papier | Fördert gute Waldnutzung
FSC® C083411

Kolibri 360 GmbH
Ferdinand-Jühlke-Straße 7
99095 Erfurt, Deutschland
produktsicherheit@kolibri360.de